PUMPKIN
Seeds of Thanks

Ed,
Class of "60" and 154 Life Brother!
Beulah Williamson

PUMPKIN

Seeds of Thanks!

Beulah Newton Williamson

Pumpkin Seeds of Thanks
Copyright 2020 by Beulah Newton Williamson

ISBN 978-1-7354010-0-3

Please note the experiences described in this memoir are true and written to the best of my recollection and interpretations. A few names and individual specifics have been changed to protect the privacy and sensitivities of the persons and families depicted. Additionally, some conversations quoted may not be the exact words spoken to me or vice-versa, but I have most certainly attempted to summarize the spirit of what was communicated.

All rights reserved. No part of this work may be reproduced or transmitted in any form, electronic or mechanical, including photocopying.

This book was printed by BCP Digital Printing
in Baltimore, Maryland.
Cover Design: Sylvester Williamson
Editing: Sharlonda L. Waterhouse
Book Design: mitchell&sennaar communications, inc.

Contents

Acknowledgments vii

Preface ix

Pumpkin's Beginnings 1

Momma's House 11

Jackie's Birth 15

14th Street Neighbors 17

Casket Lady 25

Bluing 27

Six and Done 33

Walking Into Reality 37

East Cherry Lane 45

Welcomed Change 59

Store Runner 63

Uncles	65
Red Top	71
St. Matthew United Methodist Church	75
Sollers Homes	81
Turner Station	93
Unforgettable Summers	97
Fooled	99
Momma's Choir	105
Pig Outing	109
Summer of 1955	111
Doo-doo Sandwich	115
Snowballs	119
Rocking Through Challenges	121

Acknowledgments

Looking back over my Pumpkin years of experiences, I thank Jehovah God, the Sovereign Lord of the Universe, for the countless family, friends, neighbors, and associates who have been instrumental in positively influencing my life, many of whom are celebrated within the pages of this book.

Thank you to my husband, Sylvester Williamson, "my man of strength," greatest supporter, protector, live-in comedian, as well as God's instrument of discipleship and the people's crusader. God made only one; ask any of his "other" wives, Marlene Jones, Josephine Woodard, or the former one, Deanna Fleming.

To Derick S. Williamson, my son, who overcame the calling of the streets to not only be a hand-up in helping others but more so a role model father: You put a capital "F" in "Fathering" Deria, Deja, and Derick D., along with your grandson, Dameer, and granddaughter, Demi.

To Deitra Wilson, my daughter: I admire that you are generously loving and giving; beautiful within and out; whose faith and trust in God often mirrors the strength of the Drake, Newton, and Williamson foremothers in adversity; and devoted mother of Melvin and Ahmaad.

To Nora Graham, our chosen daughter: I am so blessed that you so lovingly accepted me as your surrogate mother. Over the past 36 years, you have blossomed into a woman of character;

committed mother of Terrell Graham; and a beacon of light to underprivileged children.

I give the most profound appreciation to Vernetta Linton, Bobbie Swann, and Georgia Williamson, who freely served as reviewers. To Flavia Williams Rutkosky, my best friend since first-grade, words can never express my gratitude for the time and effort you so unselfishly gave to ensure my ***Pumpkin Seeds of Thanks*** experiences are a worthwhile read. To God be the glory!

Preface

Pumpkin's Seeds of Thanks **is a recollection of my childhood** memories and teenage interactions, as well as information I learned from overhearing adult family conversations. I often shared stories with my five siblings about my delight in growing up in Winston-Salem, North Carolina, with our grandmother Edna, whom I called "Momma." I experienced seeing my sister, Jackie, being born in the pee pot; Momma using bluing in my bathwater to lighten my skin; the doo-doo sandwich being given to a playmate; and being chased by wild pigs in the woods.

Many of these experiences are not written in chronological order, but in life chapters, as they often overlapped my stays between Winston-Salem and Turner Station, Maryland. Each chapter represents a memorable event in my childhood, youth, or teenage years. The influences of a loving family, lasting friendships, caring neighbors, committed teachers, as well as encounters with negative individuals and the finality of death formed these chapters of my young beginning.

I became inspired to share my story by my husband, Sylvester, and daughter, Deitra, who are both writers and independent filmmakers. As I began writing about these experiences, a flood of vivid memories came to mind. I relived my first six years of childhood living in Winston-Salem with Momma; my school years in Turner Station with my parents, Porter and Minnie;

and my delight in spending 11 down-the-country summers with Momma in the land of my milk and honey: Winston-Salem.

As I closed a chapter and began a new one, I became wide-eyed to realize the overarching themes of how God continuously brought me through bad to better times and better to the best of times. My gratefulness is in response to Bible scripture 1 Thessalonians 5:18 (King James Version) that states, "In everything give thanks: for this is the will of God in Christ Jesus concerning you." After each chapter, ***Pumpkin Seeds of Thanks***, express my gratitude in similarity to the abundance of seeds found in a pumpkin. Because of God's grace, mercy, and favor, I am the "me" of today. I am ever so thankful for life lessons learned from listening to those who gave me wise counsel during the formative years of my life, from a baby through age eighteen, when I was affectionately called "Pumpkin."

Pumpkin's Beginnings

Minnie Jean Jackson was birthed on a Tuesday in 1923, and Porter Newton, Jr. entered this world a year later on a Monday in 1924, in Red Springs, North Carolina. Both were raised in godly, prayer-filled homes and taught moral conduct from early childhood. Minnie was reared in the Baptist faith's religious principles, and Porter was deep-rooted as a Methodist. They were above-average students and popular stars of the boys' and girls' basketball teams at Red Springs High School. In their early teen years, they became sweethearts but were forbidden by their family heads to court. During the summer and fall, they conspired to pick tobacco and cotton on the same farms to circumvent this control. Their caring for one another was so deep that enduring daily miserable back-bending work in the scorching heat was worth it to them to be close whenever possible.

Upon graduating in 1940, Minnie attended Winston-Salem Teachers College in Winston-Salem, North Carolina. It was conveniently located near her mother's, Edna Drake Jackson Crews', home. Once Porter completed high school, he pursued his beloved Minnie, and their romance blossomed; sometime in the steamy hot summer of July 1941, I was unexpectedly conceived.

According to Minnie, the social taboos associated with the shame of having me out of wedlock were challenging for not only her but also all the family, especially her mother, Edna. Minnie had violated the moral expectations of behavior in the Holy Bible regarding premarital sex and her Baptist upbringing. As with many unwanted pregnancies during that era, I was an embarrassing dark secret that came to light when her belly bulged, disfiguring her shapely physique. When at all possible, pregnant city girls were sent to relatives in the south "down the country." Country girls were sent to relatives in the city or kept housebound until giving birth.

Minnie was tucked away for several months in Germantown, Pennsylvania, at her maternal Aunt Julia's and Uncle Reverend Henry Baldwin's home. Porter, unable to find employment, enlisted in the United States Navy. **I, Beulah Mae (Marie) Newton ("Pumpkin"),** was born on a Tuesday in the spring of 1942; Minnie was 19, and Porter, 18. Upon completing the required 30-day recuperation period after my delivery, Minnie carted me off to Winston-Salem to live with her mother, Edna. She was born on a Sunday in the summer of 1904. She was 38 years old. From the time I could talk, I called my grandmother "Momma."

Momma had two sons younger than Minnie; Hume Jr., affectionately called "Son," was 15, and Preston, called "Coot," was 13. They were raised in Red Springs by Momma's father, King George Drake, and her sister, Sallie Jane. Momma had left all three of her children with them several years before and moved to Winston-Salem to escape frequent beatings by her first husband, Hume Sr. King George, a God-fearing Christian, who vowed to cut Hume Sr.'s heart out of his chest if he ever so much as raised his hand to wave hello to Momma. In Winston-Salem, she only had responsibility for herself, but she welcomed me with open arms.

Once Momma became comfortable caring for me, Minnie moved to Washington, D.C. to live with her first cousin and best friend,

Ludella, to find work. It was the first time she lived independently of her immediate family, but with Ludella's guidance, she adapted quickly to the faster pace of city life. She obtained a clerical position in the Russian Embassy under President Franklin Delano Roosevelt's administration.

On many occasions during my teen and adult years, Minnie spoke of how World War II opened up job opportunities for Coloreds in the North, especially females in clerical areas. She always spoke reverently of President Roosevelt and how he helped provide jobs for Coloreds despite racial segregation, indefensible prejudice, and at-will lynching during that era. Time and time again, she told me of her presence among the thousands of mourners who lined the streets of D.C. for his funeral procession on April 14, 1945, and that she cried. With Porter on a ship in the Atlantic Ocean and Minnie in D.C., their visits to see me were seldom, if at all.

Momma was employed as a day worker, providing care, cleaning, and cooking services to White families with shut-in individuals; her hours were long. Fortunately, Momma was able to get Miss Mamie, who lived about four blocks away just beyond Brown's grocery store, to keep me while she worked. Miss Mamie, an elderly, snuff-dipping woman, had kept children over many years, but she was no longer a child caregiver. However, she agreed to keep me, but only temporarily until Momma found somebody, which never happened. She kept me from when I was a baby until I was six years old and during the summers until I was eleven.

Miss Mamie was tall, big-breasted and full-figured with dark, wrinkled skin from years of picking cotton in the blistering hot North Carolina sun. Her lips always looked swollen from the lump of dipping snuff packed around her bottom gum, and her breath smelled of it. She could aim that brown spit with precision into the large tin coffee can that was always sitting no less than a foot away. I was glad she did a lot of hugging on me and not kissing because of the stinky smell of her breath. Several old, faded pictures revealed she had been attractive, shapely, and kissable in her younger days.

Miss Mamie was a widow. She lived in a small, single-family home in the middle of a block of similar one-story houses. Her house had a living room, two bedrooms, a kitchen, and a bathroom. Her son, Josh T., lived nearby and checked on her daily, never leaving until after spreading his big feet under her dessert-laden kitchen table and filling his belly with the meal of the day. No matter what she cooked, boiled or fried (chicken from the coop, vegetables, pot meals of beans or pork neckbones and potatoes), those savory smells were always overpowered by the sweet smells of her baking.

White folks from miles away flocked to her flowerpot-filled wooden porch to buy gingerbread loaves; sugar cookies; and pineapple, coconut, and chocolate cakes. To their delight, Miss Mamie always gave them a little cloth sack of homemade peanut brittle with each cake.

Most of Miss Mamie's White customers picked up their orders and were quickly on their way. However, the Madison brothers always shared a pan of gingerbread and pop right at the table with me. They would express sighs of delight, rub their bellies, pay, and kiss Miss Mamie on the cheek. They would fuss over who Miss Mamie loved best. She would say, "both of you the same," and they would pretend to tussle until she playfully showed them the door. Before leaving, each brother gave me a nickel. They were White and nice; I liked them.

Pumpkin's Beginnings

Miss Mamie loved and cared for me like her own blood grandchild, overfed and spoiled me even more than Momma. I could do no wrong. Likewise, I loved and adored Miss Mamie until the day when I was about 14 years old, and she faded from her house into heaven. Other than Momma, Miss Mamie was the sweetest, most loving adult of my childhood to teen years in Winston-Salem.

It was Miss Mamie who affectionately nicknamed me "Pumpkin," and it became "my name," called by all who knew me.

ઇ • ફ

"Pumpkin Seeds of Thanks" to God for my loving parents, Porter and Minnie, who endured a difficult situation and chose not to abort, leave me on a stranger's doorstep, or give me away to other family members; the unselfish love and sacrifice of my sweet Momma to assume responsibility for my upbringing; and the blessing of my devoted angels of care, Miss Mamie and Josh T.

Pumpkin Seeds of Thanks

Father, Porter Jr.

Mother, Minnie

Grandmother, Edna

Cousin Ludella and Mother Minnie

Momma's House

Momma lived at 2021 East 14th Street in a two-story multifamily building that housed four apartments. It was built in 1920. The apartment building was in the center of a block of beautiful well-cared-for single-family homes. Metal outdoor chairs sat on each of the four porches. The front yard had grass only on the sides of the building because cars were parked in the yard. Steps, back doors, and space between the houses on both sides of the building allowed for easy access to the backyard which was a shared area for all the renters. The popular 14th Street Park was directly across the street with swings, seesaws, sliding boards, monkey bars, merry-go-round, and a huge swimming pool.

Momma and I lived on the first-floor apartment on the left of the building. It was full of stuff. A piano took up the entire center wall in the living room, and a couch, two chairs, and a floor model radio crowded out the remainder of the room. Pictures of Great-Grandpa King George Drake and Mahalia Jackson were on the walls.

The one-bedroom had a full-sized bed that was always made up, two dressers, a sewing machine laden with stacks of decorative feed sacks, a straight back chair, an overstuffed closet, and a pee pot with a lid for Momma's use during the wee hours of the morning. Along the wall of the dimly lit hall leading to the kitchen and bathroom were my rollaway bed and a trunk to store my clothes. Stacks of Momma's homemade quilts, blankets, and flattened out boxes of unused presents were permanent wall fixtures. Gifts of nightgowns, robes, slips and handkerchiefs given to her over the years were rarely used.

The kitchen had a wood stove and icebox in a cabinet, with shelves for block ice and food refrigeration. A table, four chairs, and a cabinet with open shelves for dry goods filled up the rest of the area. The enclosed porch adjacent to the kitchen was an outdoor storage room that led to the backyard and housed all kinds of stuff, including several black iron frying pans, pots, and garden tools.

The backyard belonged to all four families, but Momma claimed most of it for her rooster; chickens; two pigs in a pen with a slop trough; our dog, Jack Jack; and a vegetable garden. She shared her eggs and vegetables with the other tenants, who had no problem with her hogging most of the space as long as they had access to the shared storage shed.

Momma arose to the sound of the rooster crowing to start her house chores before dropping me off at Miss Mamie's house and going to work. After starting the fire for heating the water to wash up, she religiously made her bed and dumped and rinsed the pee pot. Once the sun heightened, Momma, being fair-skinned, shielded her face with a wide straw hat with her hair pinned up under it. She would feed the chickens, the dog, and pigs which oinked and snorted as they greedily competed to get more food scraps than the other. Momma was short and round in the mid-section but she moved fast. On Saturday afternoons, I dreaded seeing her sneak up behind a chicken, grab it with lightning speed, wring its neck with feathers flying in the air, and then, without mercy, chop its head off with the hatchet. I never understood how it could still run and flap its wings without its head.

Although I hated seeing Momma kill a chicken week after week, I had no feelings of regret at Sunday supper. I always ate a wing and thigh that Momma fried in fatback and bacon grease saved in a can on the back of the stove. With the chicken, she served string beans, field peas, collard greens, potato salad, gingerbread, or cake. It was sooo good. To top off the meal, we shared one little bottle of Coca-Cola in glasses filled to the rim with ice. As with the chickens, I became attached to the pigs, but when they were fattened, they would become my tasty breakfast meat. I loved eating Momma's cooking, best of all, her grits with country ham, pork pudding or slab bacon, and any kind of beans with buttery biscuits or cornbread.

"Pumpkin Seeds of Thanks" to God for Momma's cluttered house, which overflowed love, inviting hospitality, and finger-licking good food.

Jackie's Birth

On a winter Monday morning in February 1946, at almost four years old, I was awakened by moaning, groaning, and crying coming from Momma's bedroom. Listening closely, I realized it was Minnie, who had come to visit us for a while with a really big stomach. Something not so good was going on, and I got more and more scared and started crying because she sounded like she was about to die. I looked for answers and comfort from Porter, who had surprised us with a visit the day before, but he looked sick too. My parents had married in 1943. Porter received an honorable discharge in November 1945, and they were living in Baltimore, Maryland. He was walking back and forth, looking like he was about to throw-up. Upon the arrival of Minnie's brothers, Uncle Son and Uncle Coot, with Aunt Sallie Jane (Momma's sister), my father and uncles disappeared out the front door without a second thought of concern or comfort for my anxiousness.

Children were seen but not heard. Poor little me was told nothing. As Aunt Sallie Jane hurried back and forth to the kitchen, carrying water in a washbasin, I ran to her crying; she pushed me aside and hurried into the room with Minnie. I was so scared. Amid all that confusion, I just had to see what was going on. I peeped through the cracked door of the bedroom, which never closed tight due to the overload of Momma's Sunday clothes hanging on it. To my surprise, my pretty mother looked a mess, hair all over her head, frowning with pain, and sweating like a "runaway" pig.

Pumpkin Seeds of Thanks

Momma and Aunt Sallie Jane were telling Minnie to "push, push, push," but she was too busy hollering to listen. I wondered, push what? I was so scared and nervous, I thought my heart was going to jump out of my chest, but I could not stop peeping. Finally, after one loud scream, I saw a tiny baby covered in bloody slime pop out of her into the seed sack draped on the bucket.

Aunt Sallie Jane picked the baby up and slapped it on the butt, and it cried like a squealing piglet. The seed sack slid to the floor, and I realized that the bucket was actually the pee pot Momma used every night for the convenience of not having to walk down the long dark hall to the bathroom.

My sister, Jacqueline Cecile (Jackie), who looked like a reddish White baby, had just been born. After witnessing that event, I vowed no baby ever for me. Whatever Minnie did to get that baby, I definitely would not be doing ever in life.

Jackie cried most of the time, and I had to run for the diapers, Vaseline, and baby powder. Neighbors were constantly coming in and out, saying she was cute and making a big deal over her. Little brown me felt ugly and left out. After thirty days of recuperation, Minnie took that attention-stealing, reddish-white looking, crying baby with her to live in Baltimore, Maryland. With Jackie gone, it was all about me again. Two years and seven months passed before I saw that crying baby again.

"Pumpkin Seeds of Thanks" to God for my precious jewel of a sister, Jackie, who never accepted the fact that I witnessed her birth with all of the slimy details, especially her popping into the pee pot.

14th Street Neighbors

Mr. Hampton Haith lived at the beginning of our block on 14th Street at Cameron Avenue in a big brick house with a swimming pool. I have no memory of Mr. Haith's family. He was always hurriedly coming or going as we walked by. Momma would holler out, "How are you today, Mr. Hayes?" She pronounced Haith as Hayes, as did most of the neighbors. He would respond with, "Just fine, Miss Edna. How are you?" and say to me, "Hello Miss Pumpkin," wave, and be on his way. Momma told me, that he was a smart man who owned the busses Colored people rode on, and he had plenty money. In my late teen years, I learned that Mr. Haith was a big wheel with the Safe Bus Company, the first Colored bus transportation ownership in Winston-Salem. Because of the Safe Bus, Momma and other Coloreds no longer had to walk halfway into town to catch a city bus to get to work or wherever.

The Cook family; Mr. Cook; his wife, Miss Eva; and son, Sammy, lived next door to Mr. Haith. Not only did Mr. Cook own Cook's Shoe Shop, he also worked at a hotel downtown. Miss Eva dressed up every day like it was Sunday. Out of all the houses on the block, theirs was the one I liked best. It was a big brick two-story single house that sat back from the street in the middle of a neat grassy yard. It was eye-catching.

Sammy, who was about three years younger than me, was not allowed to leave his yard and mostly played by himself. I loved the times when several of us neighborhood kids would be invited to play croquet with him. It was different from what I was used to playing: jump rope, hopscotch, and dodge ball. Hitting the colorful balls through the hoops with the mallets on the neatly mowed lawn with Sammy dressed in his knee-breeches and long socks made me feel rich. Being spoiled, Sammy did not like to lose and would pout if any of us beat him. Therefore, to stay on his good side and keep being invited back, we learned to play the game well enough to challenge him but not beat him too often. He was happy, and so were we.

After playing the game, we were invited inside the Cooks' home to eat little sandwiches of egg salad cut into different shapes and cookies served on pretty saucers. It seemed drinking the lemonade out of the fancy pitcher, and matching glasses made it taste even better than Momma's. I daydreamed of having a house full of fancy furniture and "stuff" just like the Cooks when I grew up. I thought the Cooks were rich.

Three houses separated our apartment building from the Cooks'. Next to the Cooks were the Gaylords, who owned the Gaylords Cleaners. Next to them was Mr. Doug, who looked like a White man. From time to time, all in fun, he would drape a sheet over himself with open slits for his eyes and jump out of the bushes as I passed by, scaring me into crying laughter. Adjacent to Mr. Doug was the Moores and my playmates, Irene, Bobby, and Norma.

On the right side of our apartment building was the Lafayettes with whom I had no memorable relationship. In the house next door to them were the dark-skinned, pearly white-toothed, good-looking Colemans: Reverend and Mrs. Coleman and their children, Shirley, Pat, and my good buddy Vernon. I never knew if Dorinda and Lee, who were much older than us and lived with them, were Vernon's big sisters or aunts. When we played in the

Colemans' yard, those two ladies watched us with eagle eyes and kept us in check. At the end of the block were the Hemphills, with whom I had little contact other than friendly greetings. Selena, the daughter, was brown-skinned and pretty. Her hair was always done, and she wore beautiful clothes. I wanted to be like her when I grew up.

Across the street from the Hemphills, at the end of the park, was another family of Gaylords. They, more than likely, were related to the Gaylords who owned the cleaning business because that Mr. Gaylord drove a Gaylord's Cleaners' truck. As with the Hemphills, other than a wave or greeting, there was no close contact. The city limit ended at our street, and the winding road of thick trees led to the hog and cow farms a couple miles around the bend, which, on a North Carolina hot day, stunk to no end. Still, I was happy!

For me, of all the beautiful houses on our street, our modest apartment building was the best in which to live. We were four individual families in what seemed like one big family house.

Mr. Roy; his wife, Miss Julia Mae; and daughters, Betty Jean and Shirley, lived in the apartment above us. I had a sisterly relationship with Betty and Shirley. Miss Julia Mae was a quiet woman who chatted with the neighbors as she came and went from work but mostly kept to herself. Mr. Roy was outgoing and talkative. He drove a red truck for a flour company and delivered big sacks of flour to stores. After work, he would sit on the porch for hours talking to any and everybody who had time to listen about how many sacks he delivered that day and where. He would show off his muscles by lifting one of us kids on each arm at the same time. His loud belly-shaking laugh made me laugh.

Mr. Roy was funny most of the time; however, he transformed into a different person when he listened to professional boxing matches on the radio. For me, he became utterly scary on fight nights. It was as if he was physically in the ring with Joe Louis', Archie Moore's, Rocky Graziano's, or Sugar Ray Robinson's opponents, and he was their invisible shadow man. Mr. Roy sat in the chair or moved around the room acting out furious uppercuts, hooks, jabs, straight rights, overhand rights, and whatever other punches he could throw. He moaned and groaned when his favorite boxer got hit. At the end of the fight when his boxer won, he would parade around the living room with his arms up in victory as if he had thrown the knockout punch. It was an unbelievably creepy but hilarious scene to behold. In the event his boxer was defeated, he looked beaten and miserable for days.

The Phelps lived upstairs across from Mr. Roy's family. They were the oldest of all the neighbors but my favorites. They were retired from the R. J. Reynolds Tobacco Company. Mr. Phelps had a straight-up, no nonsense demeanor. He was a deep darkskinned, tall, thin, handsome man of proud character. He taught us to do what the "Good Book" said about loving and helping one another. He often spoke of how God cooled his temper, shut his mouth, held his fists to his sides, and allowed him to endure the wrongs and cruelty of Whites. He would grin from ear to ear with great satisfaction telling us evil people burn in hell, and surely not many White folks would make it with the rest of us. He warned us to watch out for the "White devils", who would do anything to hold us back by putting their "foot on our necks" to keep us down. He was fixed on teaching us the necessity of faith in God, education, and common sense to be successful.

Mrs. Phelps was dark-skinned, short, and thin. She dipped snuff and possessed a delightful on-the-spot sense of humor. She had a weird stiff dance move that was a combination of the itch and a snake charmer. Out of her sight, we belly-rolled, laughing, trying to imitate her moves. Her favorite quote to us kids was "Quit looking down my throat," meaning she was talking to grown folks, not us. She and Momma were all-out jokesters together, and we were often the brunt of their antics, from their scaring us as boogeymen in sheets to pretending to throw make-believe puke or snot on us.

The Phelps' grandson, Jerry, lived with them and was not a bad kid, but he was a spoiled rotten brat, who did no wrong in their sight. All he had to do was water up his big green eyes in that cute, high-yellow freckled face, and he was deemed innocent of whatever mischief he had committed. Being a little older than Jerry, I, too, thought he was a darling and ever so lovable most of the time. He pronounced my nickname "Pumpkin" in a slow country drawl that sounded like "Punnnkin."

Momma's niece, Helen, and her husband, Mr. Charles, lived on the first floor separated from us by a porch and stairs leading to the two apartments on the upper level. Helen was pretty, red bone in complexion, Coca Cola-shaped with long hair, and funny, especially when she nipped Kentucky Gentleman. Mr. Charles was much older than Helen. He was nice-looking with a light brown complexion and thick, wavy hair; he was a few inches shorter than she. He was an educated man, very proud of his schooling. He owned Millers Printing Company, which by his own words was very successful. He went to work every day dressed in a suit and tie. He kept to himself and was considered to be uppity by most neighbors. However, he was like one of my uncles to me: caring and generous. He gave me copies of the *Weekly Reader*, a weekly newspaper for elementary school children to read, and would ask me questions to make sure I had read and understood. He rewarded me with chocolate Tootsie Roll pops and bubble gum.

Mr. Charles stressed every letter of Pumpkin (not "Punkin" like most folks). I enjoyed sitting at his knee on the porch with the other children, listening to stories of his strict upbringing and education being the key to owning his business. He was so proud of not having to work for the White man. He was not only the boss but also a mentor, training other Coloreds to follow in his footsteps.

On a Thursday in 1947, Christmas day, Helen gave birth to a son, Winford, affectionately called "Winkie" by Helen. Thankfully, unlike with Jackie, I did not witness Winkie's birth. He was a cute little boy with olive-brown skin, curly hair, and the perfect placement of ears, brown eyes, nose and mouth. I loved him like a little brother.

From the ages of seven through 10, the joy of my life on summer visits to Winston-Salem was my little, third cousin, Winkie. When he was two years old, he was like a living, breathing, walking doll baby. I would put water, Royal Crown or Dixie Peach hair grease in his hair and slick it to his scalp like a processed conk. I showed it to him via a hand mirror and delighted in his giggling with approval. Most times the do only lasted an hour, so I would put him between my legs and grease it again. Looking back, I have no clue why Mr. Charles and Helen allowed me to slick his hair, except maybe it copycatted Mr. Charles' natural waves.

I loved it when Momma babysat Winkie overnight, and we shared my rollaway bed together. I would grease his hair and set the waves with a stocking cap. Afterward, I rocked him almost breathless until sleep overtook him to prevent him from removing the cap. For certain, the morning waves would be silky, curly and lasting.

He was a darling cutie. I loved myself some Winkie, and he loved me.

All four of our families were close-knit and looked out for one another, sharing whatever was needed.

⊰ • ⊱

"Pumpkin Seeds of Thanks" to God for our "home" in an apartment building that housed four families as one, for being perfectly situated "slap dab" in the middle of the block of homeowners and never knowing we were tenants, for us being a beacon of love to each other, resulting in my cherished memories of fun, fun, fun.

Thanks for Winkie, my doll baby, whom I loved and received much joy from being his hair dresser.

Also, thanks be to God for the entrepreneurial abilities of the Colored men and women on our block to rise above bias and segregation by seizing opportunities of education and business trades to better conditions for themselves as well as other Colored people.

Mrs. Phelps on Porch

East 14th Street Apartment Building (2017)

Casket Lady

At the age of five, I experienced the most terrifying moments of my young life when Momma walked me into the Hooper Funeral Home to view the body of an elderly neighbor's sister. As it was on the way to Miss Mamie's house, I was aware of dead people being laid out in there and had always been leery of walking by it. I resisted going in, but Momma forcibly took me by the hand and led me in even though I was visibly trembling. Upon entering this dimly lit, narrow room, I immediately focused on the casket, which was on a tall stand under a light, much too close for comfort. I was happy I could not see the dead lady; unfortunately for me, as people greeted and mingled, I became separated from Momma.

Next thing I knew, a man picked me up and forced me deep into the casket close enough to kiss the woman's face. She was real dead; her face was pasty dry from dark brown powder outlined by at least 100 tight grey curls all over her head, and she was stiff as a plank of wood around the pigpen.

My hollering finally alerted Momma, who was in the back of the overcrowded room having a hallelujah good time singing the woman into heaven. He continued to firmly hold me over her for what seemed like eternity until I peed on myself and him. Needless to say, he quickly put me down. I was scared beyond what words can express, and I did not go near a dead body for a long, long time.

After that horrifying experience, I had nightmares for months and began a lifetime of stuttering. From then on, while walking to Miss Mamie's, I crossed to the other side of the street in the event the door might open as I passed by. Momma realized the suffering I had experienced and was so sorry for my anguish. She constantly prayed for God to heal me of my stuttering and fear. I waited for the miracle.

✥ • ✥

"Pumpkin Seeds of Thanks" to God for allowing me to recover from such a horrific experience that without His grace may have resulted in my inability to speak and a total psychological breakdown.

Bluing

Saturday evening baths were a ritual for me at Momma's house. Momma would fill two big pots with water about midday and set them on the stove to warm from the heat of cooking breakfast and supper. Then, she put more wood on the fire and heated the warmed water until it boiled and the wood burned out. One filled pot along with the water from the faucet usually filled the tin tub halfway. Before allowing me to get in, Momma always added Little Boy Blue Bluing to the water. It was a blue liquid product for whitening clothes, sold at stores in the soap powder section. She said it was good for cleaning the week's dirt off me. Once I soaped up, she would make me scrub my elbows and knees with a brush real hard to keep them evenly toned with my complexion. She did not want me to have rusty elbows and knees like her friend Miss Mae's little granddaughter, Jenny.

Momma used the second pot of water to rinse me off and let me pretend to swim until I was shivering cold. Baths were so much fun! Once towel dried, she greased my skinny little body with lard to keep me from breaking out from the bluing. My skin would be smooth and soft, but still brown.

In my innocent heart, I knew Momma used the bluing to lighten my skin. I even hoped the bluing would work just to make her happy, but it never did. I remained as brown as ever. Momma never knew I told my friends about my "Saturday night bleaching," and they, of course, teased me about her wanting me to be lighter.

Pumpkin Seeds of Thanks

Looking back, I don't know specifically why Momma was preoccupied with skin color. I just thought, for some unspoken reason, to her lighter skin was more appealing and acceptable than darker skin. I learned years later that Momma was the product of biracial parents.

Per the writings of the Drake family historian, Ludella Stubbs Currie, Momma was one of 14 children born to her father, King George Drake, who was the color of a black cast iron frying pan, and Della Brown Drake (White). Della was the daughter of John and Mary Drake, who owned King George as a slave in Charleston, South Carolina, but for some unknown reason allowed him to marry Della. In terms of complexion, Momma's siblings were a rainbow of colors from passable White and fair-skinned to olive-brown and dark-skinned. When the older Drake children were of school age in Marlboro County, South Carolina, the family moved to Red Springs. Wise King George introduced Della to neighboring folk as being Indian (Native American) to avoid being lynched by the White man. In considering Momma's family history, there is no telling the degree of harmful negativity she may have witnessed growing up with her rainbow of siblings, especially the darker ones. Apparently, her life experiences determined in her mind that there were certainly advantages to being light-skinned in the White world as well as the Colored. Being light-skinned and working for White folks, she was very color conscious.

◈ ● ◈

"Pumpkin Seeds of Thanks" to God for allowing me to come to believe Psalm 139:14 (New King James Version): "I will praise You, for I am fearfully and wonderfully made; Marvelous are Your works, and that my soul knows very well."

Great-Grandfather, King George

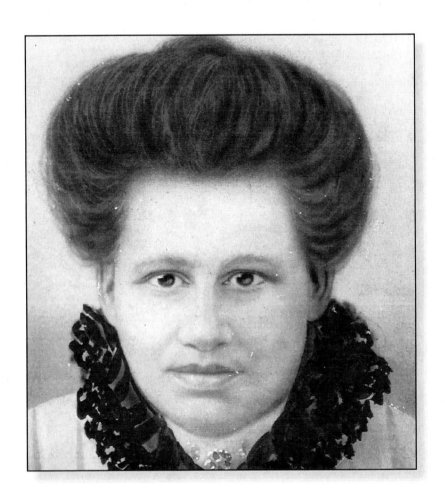

Great-Grandmother, Mary

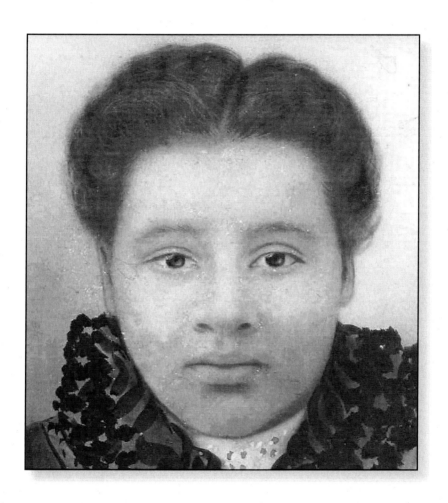

Grandmother (Momma as a Teenager)

Six and Done

Before I turned six years old, Momma took me to the Fourteenth Street Colored Grade School, which was minutes from our house, to register me for the coming school year. To our surprise and disappointment, we were informed that I would not be able to attend public school in North Carolina because Momma was not my legal guardian. My parents, Minnie and Porter, were residents/taxpayers of Maryland, so I would have to attend school in the state where they lived. What a letdown; we both cried. Momma prayed with me day and night for God to make a way for me to stay, but His answer was "no." Neither Momma nor Minnie and Porter could afford to pay out-of-state tuition. I thought my parents were mean and hated them for not making a way for me to stay with Momma and go to school with my friends. My dreams of running the short distance up and across 14th Street to the Fourteenth Street Colored Grade School were crushed, as were my likely attendance at nearby Atkins High School and Winston-Salem Teachers College.

There were a lot of calls between Minnie and Momma that made Momma cry, but I had no clue that in a few months, I would be having an emotional parting with her, Uncle Coot, Miss Mamie, and my friends. With teary goodbyes, they sent me off with candy, gingerbread, sugar cookies, and fried chicken packed in a shoebox plus my favorite root beer pop. Miss Mamie gave me snuff-filled kisses, paper dolls, coloring books, and crayons. When Mr. Wilton, a family friend who Uncle Son hired to drive us to Maryland drove into the yard, I clung to Momma crying uncontrollably. Uncle Son put my suitcase with all my worldly possessions into the trunk of the car and slammed it close. It was a sad day. My heart was broken. With a toot of the horn and wave of goodbye, we began the long journey via Route 301 to Maryland. Uncle Son did not permit me to drink my pop because welcome stops for Coloreds at gas stations were far apart, and pulling over on the side of the road had to be "quick and fast" to avoid trouble with police or evil White men. I cried most of the way.

Even though I only knew Porter and Minnie from one or two visits and quick calls, my arrival to their house was loving and welcoming. Adjustment to my new life was not easy. I went from being an only child to being one of three. Cry-baby Jackie was over two years old, and Minnie had birthed another baby, my brother, Porter III (Bay Bay), almost 16 months. He was born on a Thursday in the spring of 1947. He was light-skinned, like Jackie, with a redness in his complexion; had light green eyes and a long peanut-shaped head, like Porter; and sported tight curly hair. I was fascinated by his adorable cuteness. He was a good little boy, not a crier. I thought Minnie was mean. Her constant "do this, do that," got on my nerves. Porter never made any comments one way or another but would wink at me during Minnie's fussing spells, and he would offer me an encouraging smile to hang in there.

I missed Momma so much. Due to the cost of long-distance phone calls, we only talked once a month for a quick minute or two. At the end of those calls, I was sad and withdrawn, wanting no bother from anyone, especially Minnie. Eventually, I came to know this life was it, no returning to my "only me" life with Momma. Minnie shared with Momma how badly I was behaving, and she

Six and Done

promised if I would be a good girl, I could come to Winston-Salem after school ended the next year.

Momma's promise was all I needed to hear. My whole negative attitude changed. I became determined that absolutely nothing was going to get in the way of my going to Winston-Salem the coming summer. I drew closer to Porter and Minnie and played willingly with Jackie. I became the dutiful daughter helping with Bay Bay, doing chores, and participating in family activities. Playmates became friends, and adult neighbors spoke highly of me as being mannerly and respectful. I played the game well. Even I liked me.

All was going well until one evening when Minnie told me to come in from playing with my playmates with plenty of daylight left. I had gotten on her last nerve being a nuisance running in and out of the house too often for water and to pee. Not wanting to spoil Bay Bay like Jackie, who was a crying lap sitter, once Minnie fed and bathed him, she put him in the crib in my parent's front bedroom for the night.

Being mad and bored with looking out the window at my peers having fun, my attention zeroed in on Bay Bay. He was sleeping contently in the crib when I noticed his toenails seemed a bit long. I had seen Minnie bite his finger and toenails to shorten them. However, I was not about to put his toes in my mouth and decided to cut them. Not finding any scissors, I looked in the medicine cabinet and found just what I needed: a razor blade.

Through the slats of the crib, I grabbed hold of Bay Bay's foot to cut his nails. He responded with jerking his foot back, and I nicked him a couple or three times. He started to bleed, so I tiptoed into the bathroom for toilet paper to wipe it. By the time

Pumpkin Seeds of Thanks

I got back to him, spatters of fresh beet red blood were all over his face, arms, legs, blanket, and crib from his kicking. I tried to quiet his crying, but he would not stop. I freaked out and tiptoed to my room, hid the razor blade in Jackie's drawer, prayed "Jesus, please don't let him die," and got in bed fully dressed.

I heard Minnie tell Porter to check on Bay Bay and he answered, "He's alright, let him be; he'll fall back to sleep." By his continued panicky cry, Minnie knew something was out of the ordinary and insistently told Porter "Either you go or I will." Needless to say, with each step he took, my heart nearly pounded out of my chest. I was terrified. He turned on the light and hollered, "Oh, my God!," and called Minnie. She hurried up the stairs and screamed in horror at the frightening sight of Bay Bay covered in blood from head to toe. Once they cleaned him up and determined he was only bleeding from surface toe cuts, it was "on" to poor me, who tried to play dead. I confessed my unintentional guilt and cried more than Jackie ever did. Although they believed me, I got my first and only "don't ever do that again beating" from Porter because Minnie was too upset to do so without killing me. Thankfully, after a visit to Dr. William C. Wade (resident doctor in Turner Station), Bay Bay was determined to have only minor surface cuts and required no further medical treatment.

"Pumpkin Seeds of Thanks" to God for reconciling me to loving supportive parents and the blessing of my siblings; knowing my heart and allowing my precious baby brother, Bay Bay, to survive his first pedicure; and for his forgiving spirit toward me when he was old enough to understand that I truly loved him, and no harm was intended.

Walking Into Reality

On my first day of school at Fleming Elementary, I was more than ready to learn. However, the socialization aspect of meeting so many new peers at once was overwhelming; it was hard for me to keep still or quiet. My teacher Mrs. Owens was dark brown with dark hair, medium build, average height with high heels, and an extremely neat and nice-looking appearance. She was stern, hollered a lot, and, in my first-grade opinion, was not a nice person. I considered her to be strict because she disciplined my new friend Flavia and me numerous times a day for talking. In spite of my challenging stuttering, I loved to talk and so did Flavia.

Mrs. Owens would have us ball up our little delicate fists and crack our tender knuckles with her weapon of choice: a long, thick, dark green pencil. She had an arsenal of pencils, and we, along with Julia and Meredith (Mert), were disciplined with a great number of them due to our so-called whispering when we thought she was not looking. Even with the strict no-nonsense disciplining, she was, without a doubt, an excellent teacher who gave us a solid foundation for learning, achieving, being comfortable in our own abilities, and obeying authority.

Momma was true to her promise of letting me come for the summer if I was a good girl. The day after school closed in June 1949, Uncle Coot arrived to spend a few days with the family before taking me back down the country. The day of our trip, he was dressed in a suit, tie, and hat. I wore a brand-new green and blue suit ensemble with a white sweater that Uncle Coot bought for my trip and black patent leather Sunday shoes with white socks. I was so excited. Upon entering the bus, I headed for the first empty seat I saw to sit by the window. Uncle Coot quickly jerked me by the hand and led me past several seats that were available in the front and mid-section all the way to the back of the bus to sit in seats designated for "Colored Only."

Upon arriving in Richmond, Virginia to change busses, I walked in front of Uncle Coot following the White people into the service area. He pulled me by my shoulder and ushered me to the side of the building with a restroom and water fountain marked "Colored Waiting Room." I asked Uncle Coot why we couldn't go with the White people in the first door. I will never forget the sadness in his eyes and hunching of his shoulders as he said, "Baby, that's just the way it is." He lowered his head to indicate there was nothing he could do about it. I felt sad for both of us.

As I look back, I felt my first dislike for White folk on that bus experience. With my young eyes, I could see, without a doubt, that Uncle Coot was cleaner, neater and certainly much better dressed than those overall-wearing, tobacco-chewing White men who looked like they ran straight from the farm to the bus. I did not understand how they could think they were better than us because of the whiteness of their skin.

Subsequent to that incident, while visiting Momma that summer, we went to a segregated movie theatre downtown where White folk were admitted downstairs, and Coloreds entered via the side door to the stairs leading to the balcony. It took all the strength I had in me not to throw popcorn and pop down on them; however, I obeyed Momma's warnings to avoid trouble with them no matter what happened. Like she always said, "Even when they are wrong as two left shoes, they still think they are right because they have white skin."

Although Momma was subjected to racism, sharing my hateful feelings about White people with her got me nowhere. She attempted to live the commands of the Bible by turning the other cheek and loving everybody like Jesus. Then, too, being a light-skinned woman, she was more accepted by White folk than darker Coloreds. As she was still bathing me with bluing to lighten my brown skin, I knew she definitely had a thing about skin color.

My traumatic bus experience to Winston-Salem was still fresh in my mind on the return trip to Baltimore. Once called to board from the "Colored Only" waiting room, I followed Uncle Coot without a "why" to the back of the bus. After that demeaning experience, whenever possible, my uncles and parents made a way for me to travel by car to Winston-Salem. I was spared being made to feel less valued than White folk by bus demarcations of "White" and "Colored only."

Regrettably, I do not recall second grade. I believe Miss Hackett, who was light brown-skinned, attractive, and slender with a pageboy hairstyle, was my third-grade teacher. However, I cannot recall any details of the class. Probably because no memorable cracking of my knuckles was doled out to me, or I was more obedient.

Mrs. Thornton, who taught third grade, was not my teacher but my role model. She was light-skinned and very attractive; with the height of a model, she walked with perfect posture. I would imitate her walk by balancing a book on my head and walking erect. She had the most striking salt and pepper hair, which was cut into a stylish short bob that was just stunning. I hoped my three every-which-away plaits would grey just like hers when I grew up. She was always friendly toward me, beamed a warm smile when I encountered her, and treated me like I was special. I would mouth a big snagged-toothed grin and blush all over myself. I selfishly made sure she saw me every day. I thought her oldest daughter, Natalie, was the luckiest girl in the world to not only call her Mom but reap the benefits of having additional teaching at home.

By fourth grade, my stuttering had become a hindrance to my class participation. I experienced great difficulty in saying my name, expressing my thoughts, and answering questions. I took what seemed like forever to complete a sentence. I would get stuck on certain letter words like "b" for Beulah and "h" for hello, causing long pauses and repetitions. I was anxious and embarrassed speaking in class before the sometimes giggly classmates with their impatient stares. There were times when I wanted to hide in a closet or become invisible. I prayed constantly that God would let me speak without stuttering.

Even so, fourth and fifth grades were my best two years of elementary school. Due to the excess numbers of fourth graders, the cream-of-the-crop students from other fourth grade classes (who had the potential to achieve) were given to Miss Sembly to lessen her burden of having to teach two grade levels. She was darling, light-skinned, plump, cuddly, warm, and caring like Momma. For me, Miss Sembly was a God-sent angel. She was empathetic to my struggle and spent extra time encouraging me. Based on my written assignments, she considered me to be smart. She told me to speak more slowly and gave me several thicker pencils (yellow not green) to grip tightly in my lap. I broke many pencils. Additionally, she suggested that I tightly clutch the top of my desk as I spoke to relieve my tension and not stutter. I never understood how I could sing without stuttering and often wished

I could sing my answers, but I knew the class would have roared in laughter.

Upon returning home from Momma's at the end of summer 1952, I could not wait to see Miss Sembly. I was thrilled to learn that both Flavia and I were assigned to continue with Miss Sembly in her fifth-grade class. I had also acquired another best friend in fourth grade, Barbara (Boo). She was cute, had light brown skin, and wore every hair in place. She was always neatly dressed and funny. She was one of 12 children who were raised by a widowed mother, Mrs. Seawell. I was fascinated by Mrs. Seawell's wisdom, strength, spotless clean house, and ability to keep all those sons and daughters in check with loving discipline and individual responsibilities. When she caught Boo and me on the porch, grinning at boys passing by, she would say to stay away from those little crumb snatchers until we graduated from college and then to only marry a man with money. Boo was straitlaced and no-nonsense just like her. We not only played but studied together. I loved her as a sister.

My most memorable time with Boo was our performance in a Christmas play, standing on boxes singing *Silent Night*. Miss Sembly gave us "no pitch," "no tone" and "no voice" girls individual lead parts and we were so proud. There were eight of us in the choir. Boo and I practiced our individual parts after school at her house. On the day of the program, we were freshly scrubbed with our hair curled into pony tails and dressed in black skirts and red sweaters. We sang from the bottom of our bellies to the top of our lungs, and we did well. I was moved to tears and never forgot the wonder of that day. "Silent night, holy night" was not silent that day. It became my favorite Christmas carol.

There was a disruptive fourth grade student named Leon in Miss Sembly's combined class of fourth and fifth graders that year.

He was deep dark-skinned and had a lazy eye. He was a mean, rebellious knuckle-head who sparked fear in even the toughest boys. He had an uncontrollable temper. From the beginning of the school year, he religiously picked on me, called me skinny and buck-toothed, and mimicked my stuttering. I dreaded his presence. How he was chosen for Miss Sembly's class was always a mystery to me because he showed no attention to learning. He disrupted the class several times throughout the day, and most of the class was terrified of him. Obedience to authority may have been a part of his home training, but he definitely did not practice it in school.

I vividly remember Miss Sembly reprimanding Leon one morning for refusing to stay in his seat. As she approached him, he cussed, and tussled her to the floor. I and others jumped in to help her, and he threatened to take the entire class on. He was strong as an ox, and it took two male teachers to physically remove him to the principal's office. To my delight, he was suspended and absent for a good while.

Upon Leon's return, I was amazed that Miss Sembly warmly welcomed him and treated him as if nothing had happened. I had learned in Sunday School to turn the other cheek, but her example was mind-blowing. Not me, I was not about to be nice; I hated him and that was that.

The end of the school year was bittersweet. I passed to the sixth grade, but leaving Miss Sembly made me so sad. I think she felt the same about me. She considered me one of her successes because I had become more participatory and confident under her guidance. As we said our goodbyes, she whispered in my ear, " Remember, no matter what stumbling blocks you face because of stuttering, the only way to overcome is to keep on trying until you are understood." We parted with warm hugs and lots of tears. She was a gifted teacher. I never stopped loving her.

ஒ • ஓ

"Pumpkin Seeds of Thanks" to God for the role model teachers at Fleming Elementary School, who were committed to imparting knowledge as well as effective discipline to widen my possibilities in the world. More so, thanks for the love and encouragement of Miss Sembly, who motivated me to overcome my fear of speaking in public because of my stuttering.

Also, thanks to God for my surviving the impact of prejudicial Jim Crow laws and occurrences of personal acts of racism. Those experiences gave me insight as to how to cope and mask my feelings with White folk, who because of the brownness of my skin, treated me as inferior; lessons well-learned.

East Cherry Lane

Of all the communities in Turner Station, Carver Homes, Earnest Lyon Homes, Old Turners (referred to as Up Top), Turner Homes, The Meadow and Sollers Homes, I was glad I lived in Day Village. Growing up in that community for six years was an enjoyable childhood experience. It was a neighborhood of neat brick townhouses with small individual, manicured lawns and concrete steps. We lived at 107 East Cherry Lane in a block of six connected townhouses near the rear of the complex.

Our house had a combined living and dining room area and a compact kitchen on the first floor with front and backdoor entrances. On the second floor were two bedrooms and a bath. Our front door faced the Circle Pond set in an open field lined with large Weeping Willow trees. Juniper Lane was in the back of us surrounded by water near the picnic and beach area. We were repeatedly cautioned not to go near the pond or the water at the end of the block and in the rear. As most of us could not swim and feared drowning, we heeded the warning. On hot summer evenings, Minnie frequently walked us to the beach area to cool off by putting our feet in the water. I listened to the ripple of the waves and wondered how the fish could sleep with all that noisy motion. I also wondered why God created mosquitoes.

On Sundays, White people, as if in a parade, took slow moving car rides through Day Village down North Avondale Road (main street) back to the waterfront of Peach Orchard Lane. Unknown to my playmates and me, we were exceedingly blessed as children to be living on beautiful waterfront property that Whites obviously enjoyed touring. Additionally, we had direct-to-the backdoor services from the ice cream man, the milk man, Mr. George Mondie's Cleaners, and Mr. Leon, the arabber. I loved to hear Mr. Leon holler "Watermelon, watermelon red, red to the rind, oh red!" as he walked with his horse drawn wagon full of fresh vegetables and fruits and to see the neighbors hurry outside to buy.

I met my sweet Granddaddy Jesse Porter shortly after I arrived in Turner Station. He was 55 and born on a Monday in July 1893. He was the patriarch of the Newton clan. I loved him from the moment he hugged me and pinched my nose. He always visited us on Sunday afternoons. I vividly remember being outside with playmates when one of them pointed to a man walking quite a distance away saying, "Here comes your grandfather." I looked and said, "That man ain't my grandfather; he is too dark. I don't know that man." As the man got closer, much to my surprise, I saw it was my granddaddy, and I was embarrassed that I had not recognized him as well as disowned him. I ran to him crying and confessed to him what I had said to my playmates. He hugged me and laughingly agreed that I did not tell a "story" (lie) and said, "I am dark." He told me not to fret that his mother always told him, "The darker the berry, the sweeter the juice." With all my color-conscious upbringing, I had never seen my Granddaddy as dark-skinned. I only saw he was good-looking with a constant, wide grin; was short with a small frame; and had a peanut-shaped head like my father, Porter.

Granddaddy was the "go to man" in our family and always came through for us in a bind. When times were financially hard for us because the Bethlehem Steel Corporation was on strike or Porter had lost money gambling, Minnie would give me a note to take to Granddaddy to borrow needed dollars. Never once did he say "no." No matter where I found him — at Aunt Menyon's house, on one of his gracious female companion's porches, or cleaning the church, — he was quick to slide his hand in his right pants pocket and count the requested amount of money out to me. If he was short of what was needed, we walked to his boarding house and got the money from his stash. In addition to being a dedicated worker at the Bethlehem Steel Corporation Pipe Mill in Sparrows Point, Granddaddy hit the "numbers game" quite often. Upon giving me the money, he pinched my nose in a loving gesture, gave me a quarter, and gave me a reassuring hug. On Porter's pay day, Minnie always gave me a white envelope with the borrowed money amount to repay Granddaddy. She was faithful in paying off her loans and trusted by Granddaddy to do so. Every now and then when she hit the "numbers game" for 5 or 10 cents, she paid him back early. He would see me coming, and we both grinned from ear to ear.

As I grew older, I learned that Granddaddy was a father among fathers. The loss of his wife, Lillie, at 33 during childbirth, along with their eighth child, Minnie Lee, two months later, devastated him. With only a third-grade education, he was left with seven children to rear on his own. He contemplated suicide several times during that period, but his Christian upbringing would not permit him to do so. As cotton and tobacco farming on the family land in Red Springs was not profitable enough to support his children, he moved to Maryland to find work. He left four sons and a daughter with his mother and sister, a daughter and son in Lillie's brother's and uncle's care, and his oldest son from a relationship before marriage with his matriarchal family.

Pumpkin Seeds of Thanks

Granddaddy sent money bi-weekly to his mother, Mattie, for the support of his children until they were grown. To his surprise, at Mattie's 100th birthday celebration at the homestead, she presented him with a check that totaled all but the first year's money that he had sent over the years. Knowing her son was heartbroken to the point of not wanting to live without his precious Lillie, Mattie wisely believed the financial support of his children would give him a reason to live, and it did.

In addition to Porter Jr., Granddaddy's daughter, Menyon, and sons, Rodney, Jessie and Malien, relocated within the Baltimore area to be closer to their father. Until then, they only saw him once a year during his one-week summer vacation or at a funeral in Red Springs. He never remarried.

Newton family and church gatherings with Granddaddy present allowed me the opportunity to develop a wealth of loving memories of him. Three in particular were his giving spirit, affectionate "hello ugly," greetings, and gentle pinching of my nose. I loved him!

All of the neighbors on East Cherry Lane were fond of Granddaddy. His presence and broad smile lit up the block. He was warmly welcomed by our neighbors who cared for each other, looked out for one another, and knew everybody else's business. In our immediate block were the Miles', Thomas', O'Neal's, Newton's (ours), and Esau's households (forgot his last name), as well as the Mandy families. Our family had a very close relationship with the Miles and Mandy families, who lived on opposite ends of the block.

In the Miles family were the father, Mr. Hus; mother, Miss Peaches; and children, Sylvia, Janet and Hawkie. They were friendly, welcoming, and had a rocking good time house. Sylvia was older, attractive, into the books, and dripped in natural sophistication. As with Selena on 14th Street in Winston-Salem, I admired Sylvia a lot. I wanted to be like her when I grew up, but Janet was my hanging buddy. She was witty like her mother, but possessed her father's natural fun side of impromptu jokes and rhythmic dance. Hawkie was Bay Bay's age and friend; they were mischievous together, bordering on bad.

Card games (poker, skin, tonk) were a form of weekend recreation, and they were held mostly at the Miles' house or ours. I preferred their house because the people not only played cards but also partied, dancing, drinking and eating chicken and pig feet sandwiches all night long.

All of us card players' kids were placed in an upstairs bedroom. When they fell asleep, I would position myself at the top of the landing of the steps, to peep between the banisters down into the living room. They partied back, talking, laughing and dancing nonstop to the rhythm of Fats Domino, Ruth Brown, and BB King. However, the most "get down" gyrations resulted from Lloyd Price's "Lawdy Miss Clawdy." I just loved seeing everybody in that low crouching position, swaying their bodies and popping their fingers. During that song, I did not have to jump up and run because somebody needed to use the bathroom. Even the card players holding tight to their money stood at the table, singing and moving to the music. When necessary, I would pretend to be asleep when Mr. Hus tiptoed into the bedroom for a refill of Kentucky Gentleman, Old Crow, and Gordons Gin from his stash in the closet. He and Miss Peaches got down.

On the other hand, I thought poker games at our house were boring. Porter was respectful of the neighbors and fearful of a police raid, so players spoke quietly while betting, winning or arguing, and there was no music. Minnie sold chicken and pork chop sandwiches, beer, bourbon, scotch, and gin. The breakfast crowd got grits, scrambled eggs, biscuits, and country slab bacon. The bacon was generally a treat given to Jackie and me by Porter's good buddy Mr. Dasher, who we called "Uncle." I loved bacon and did not appreciate it being fed to the players, but had no say in the matter. It was a money-making set-up as long as Porter only manned the table, took the house cut, and did not play.

One night in the wee hours of the morning, Jackie, Bay Bay, and I awoke to the sounds of chaos: chairs falling, folks scrambling, and police commands of "halt, don't move." We were terrified as Mr. Sam, one of the gamblers, ran into our room and crawled underneath our bed. We pulled the covers over our heads when the police turned on the light in our bedroom. They quickly closed the door and were about to head back downstairs when Jackie hollered, "A man is under our bed!" They pulled Mr. Sam from under the bed by his feet and handcuffed him. He winked and smiled at us as he was led out. We were so scared.

After things got quiet, Jackie, Bay Bay, and I tiptoed downstairs to find Minnie picking up chairs and straightening up the dining room, which was in total disorder. The police had taken Porter but thankfully not Minnie because we would have been left home alone. Of course, Jackie boo-hooed, not knowing if Porter would ever come back again. I was upset but quickly calmed down by the sight of all denominations of dollar bills scattered on the floor and under the table. I counted, recounted and stacked money.

Porter came home the next day with Mr. Sam, who laughingly told Porter and Minnie how he almost got away. He gave all three of us a dollar to make up for scaring us. Needless to say, I no longer considered poker games at our house boring.

Mr. Hus had several siblings, who were cut from the same cloth of "let the good times roll." I especially liked his sisters, Miss Anna and Pearline (Pearl). Pearl would not allow us to call her Miss Pearl, just Pearl. With her, formality was not necessary. She was a nice-looking, light-skinned busty woman. Pearl fixed up pretty when she felt like it, but for the most part was straight up, no frills. What you saw, you got.

We were not exposed to foul language and were shocked to hear Pearl's "dirty mouth." She cussed every other three words. I remember her complimenting Bay Bay at the age of about six as looking just like Porter and being a "GD" cute little "MF." On at least three instances as Porter was walking toward the house, Bay Bay fell while running to greet him and received stitches on his forehead, hand, and leg, respectively. Pearl commented that Minnie needed to lock that clumsy little MF in the house until F------ Porter arrived or have him come in the F------ back door. Minnie asked her time and time again not to cuss in our presence, but it was hopeless. Apart from her colorful language, she was a humorous, good soul and one of Minnie's closest friends.

Miss Anna was a gorgeous, light-skinned, full-figured, well-groomed lady with never a hair out of place and always dressed to the "nines." Her bubbly personality made me feel happy just being in her midst. She was street smart and had an aura of independence and strength. I will forever remember her as our "personal shopper." A day or two before Easter when Jackie and I were about seven and eleven, she came to our house with two light green, olive trim suits and black patent leather shoes in our perfect sizes. They were from an upscale department store in downtown Baltimore. Even in the days of Jim Crow, Miss Anna had connections. We jumped around like little happy bunnies because Miss Anna had made our dreams come true with those beautiful outfits.

Miss Anna told us to strut it on Easter Sunday, and that we did. With fresh curled pony tails and straight bangs, not only did we walk to St. Matthew United Methodist Church but also all over Turner Station. We visited Grand Uncle Fred, Grand Aunt Barbara, and cousins Leonard and Lenora on Avondale Road; Granddaddy Porter who lived behind them on Walnut Avenue; Uncle Jimmy and Aunt Menyon in Ernest Lyon Homes; and friends in Sollers Homes, walking until our feet hurt. We took our suits off to eat Minnie's scrumptious dinner of ham, macaroni and cheese, greens, homemade rolls, sweet potato pie, pineapple-coconut cake, and Kool-Aid. After putting our suits back on, we strolled up and down our block until evening. It was a glorious day!

As previously mentioned, next door to the Miles family were Mr. and Mrs. Thomas. They were pleasant but stayed to themselves for the most part. They were the first on our block to have a television set. It was a small screen in a big wooden brown cabinet. All the children on the block would gather on their steps shared by the adjacent neighbors, the O'Neals (playmates Vivian and Bo), peering through their screen door to watch Milton Berle on the "Texaco Star Theatre," "Amos and Andy," "Jack Benny" and "Howdy Doody," a children's program. Although the reception would fade in and out at the most inopportune time, we were fascinated to watch the shows. We were thankful the Thomases were so generous in sharing their good fortune.

Mr. Esau, Miss Johnsie, Bad Gal, Peewee, and their dog, Spider, were on the right of us, later followed by the second family to live there, the Holleys (playmates Irvin and Palsy). On Juniper Lane, in the rear were sisters Betty Ann and Jean; a few doors down from them were Luther and his "neighborhood watch" grandmother, Miss Sarah. She kept all of us kids in check, and we obeyed her correction with no back talk. Other playmates included Dorothy, Lil Gil, Danny, Dion, and Dino.

The Mandys lived in the end house with plenty of play space between them and the adjacent block. They called me "Punkin." Mr. Mandy was a chef, who worked in Ocean City during the summer and in the immediate area during the winter. During the union strikes at Bethlehem Steel Corporation, he was a good source of quality food in hard times. Miss Juanita, his wife, was pretty, friendly and immaculate as a housekeeper. Although short in stature, she was tough as nails, when necessary, and had no problem correcting our naughty behavior or reporting it to our parents.

The Mandys' oldest, Charles, was the big brother of Juanita and Maria, who were Jackie's closest friends. All of them were outgoing, well-dressed, and neat like their parents. Although only two years older than me, Charles, at times, acted as if I were a younger sister under his authority. He knew the best way to do everything, which was only his way, not my way. He and I got into a scuffle during a disagreement, and I sustained a scar near my left eye, which showed for years. Likewise, for years, he lied and blatantly denied causing it. Even so, we remained friends.

Other than with Charles, the only other childhood tussle I had was with Betty Ann (mentioned previously from Juniper Lane), who approached me because she felt I thought I was cute. I knew she had to be crazy because that thought never crossed my mind. Maybe she thought so, but with my crooked teeth, dark-skin, and nappy hair, I thought "totally not cute" was more befitting. Not sure who won, but I held my own. I was a peacemaker, not a fighter.

I do not recall celebrating Christmas growing up with Momma during the first five years of my life nor any mention of Santa Claus. Why, I do not know, for she was a shouting Baptist, not a Jehovah's Witness. I only learned of Christmas celebrating the birth of Jesus and Santa Claus bringing the toys down the chimney once I moved in with Porter and Minnie. He would go out on Christmas Eve and bring back a tree for Minnie to decorate with lights, bulbs, and garland. Under her careful watch, she let Jackie, Bay Bay, and me put the glass nativity scene under the tree and bulbs and icicles on the branches as far as we could reach. We would place homemade sugar cookies and hot cocoa on the dining room table with a note to Santa Claus about how good we had been that year and go to bed.

One Christmas when I was eight and Jackie was four, I experienced the most extraordinary Christmas of all. I saw Santa Claus!! It was on a clear moon-lit Christmas Eve about 1:00 AM. I had been determined to catch Santa Claus delivering our presents and stayed awake listening, watching and waiting for him to come to our house. I knew once it got dark, he delivered toys to children all over Baltimore. My heart was beating fast with the anticipation that he would soon be coming to Turner Station and then to us at East Cherry Lane.

All of a sudden, to my utter surprise, as I looked out our bedroom window, I saw Santa Claus. He was real as real could be. Just like in his pictures, he was wearing a red and white stocking hat with a matching suit. I looked out just in the nick of time to see him in the sleigh driven by reindeers as he was riding over the rooftop of the end house on Juniper Lane. His right arm was guiding the reins, and his left arm was waving forward as if he was on to the next stop. I could not believe my eyes. I had not heard anything: no "ho, ho, ho," no reindeer galloping, nor any movement downstairs whatsoever.

I immediately woke Jackie up to see what I was seeing, but by the time she was able to focus, Santa Claus was gone. Understandably, she cried because she missed the opportunity of a lifetime. I quietly tiptoed her downstairs to make sure he had stopped at our house, and, sure enough, he had. Under the tree were a little, hard plastic white doll with brownish hair for Jackie and a bigger white blonde doll for me, a set of pink and white dishes for us to share, and coloring books with crayons. Also, under the tree were brown paper bags with an apple, orange, nuts and hard candy for each one of us. Bay Bay had a Lionel train set with two cars on the tracks, arranged around the base of the tree plus a truck and a little car. Santa Claus had quietly come, eaten the cookies, drank the cocoa, and put toys, fruit, and candy under the tree. How I failed to hear all that going on, I will never know. However, for sure, I do know that I was so thankful to see Santa Claus in the sleigh with the reindeer riding over the rooftops of Juniper Lane; and I will forever remember my joy of that moonlight sighting.

One of my fondest memories on East Cherry Lane was having my first birthday party when I turned 10. I invited my favorite cousins, Merriel, Maxine and Joan; my neighborhood playmates, Janet and Cynthia; and my best friend and classmate, Flavia. In addition to the hot dogs, birthday cake and vanilla ice cream, Minnie made it festive with hats, balloons, and blow whistles. After the happy birthday song, I opened my gifts and liked all of them. However, Flavia's gold necklace with a charm made me giggle with delight. I had not ever owned a piece of jewelry and was thrilled to receive it, especially from Flavia. It was so beautiful. I immediately fastened it around my neck and wore it for years. After all the kids went home, I spread my gifts on the couch and admired them one by one. I was so happy.

One day, "Lawdy Miss Clawdy" by Lloyd Price came on the radio as Cynthia, my friend from across the street on North Avondale Road, and I were sitting on the couch playing with cut-out dolls. Being silly, I quickly ran upstairs and stuffed my slip and skirt in my bloomers for a big butt and gyrated the low crouch dance at the top of the stairs. I was on stage getting down, and she was belly-roll laughing until Minnie caught me. As Cynthia made a bee-line out the door, Minnie grabbed a nearby switch, bolted up the steps, grabbed me by my shoulders in a firm hold, and lit fire to my conveniently exposed legs. In between licks and breaths, she repeated "Don't ever let me catch you doing that again," as if I would.

Overall, I conducted myself in a "good girl" manner but every now and then "the Minnie" came out of me, and I would react stubbornly or hot headedly. It was then that I was disciplined to the point of what is now legislated as "child abuse." Minnie sent me to get countless switches off the Weeping Willow trees, which were conveniently lined up in the field not far from our house. If I brought back a thin flimsy one, I was sent back for three, and they were plaited. I cried going and coming knowing the pain and subsequent stinging my little legs were about to endure. My legs always welted from the whippings, and I learned many a lesson "not to do that again," and by the grace of God, I survived.

Through it all, I had the richest, fun-filled childhood imaginable: playing marbles, jacks, dodge ball, red line in-red line out, jump rope, and hide and seek with my neighboring playmates. The six townhouses on East Cherry Lane provided me the closeness and comradery of neighbors similar to that of the four-family apartment building in Winston-Salem.

"Pumpkin Seeds of Thanks" to God for the close-knit neighbors of East Cherry Lane and my unforgettable playmates who instilled in me a willingness and desire to become a positive spirit of our immediate neighborhood.

For blessing my tender years with my loving, kind-hearted, gentle, ever so generous and God-fearing granddaddy. As suggested in Deuteronomy 6:6-9, Granddaddy walked with God on his heart and shared his knowledge of faith with the young and the old. He was a true role model for all fathers!

For the extraordinary Christmas of wonder that I believed to be true and the sacrifices my parents made to give Jackie, Bay Bay, and me Christmases of Jesus' love and togetherness.

Pumpkin, Jackie and Bay Bay

Granddaddy, Porter, Sr.

Welcomed Change

Bragg Elementary was located in Sparrows Point about six plus miles from Turner Station. I had to walk less than four tenths of a mile to the Ernest Lyon Homes community to catch the school bus. I enjoyed socializing with classmates waiting for the bus regardless of the weather. I always took a window seat to look at the people walking the streets and admire the makes and colors of cars driving alongside the bus or passing us by. I particularly liked the different structural design of houses and the scenery along the route. It excited me to travel across the bridge over Bear Creek. I could see the looming, massive smoke stacks releasing dark smoke into the air from the Bethlehem Steel Corporation.

My father, Porter Jr., Granddaddy Porter, his brother (my Grand Uncle Fred), neighbors, and so many other fathers of my friends worked at either the Sparrows Point Bethlehem Steel Company, Shipyard, Pipe or the Tin Mill located in Sparrows Point, Maryland (the Point). Porter worked swing shift at the Tin Mill and, having no car, rode the #26 streetcar the short ride across Bear Creek to the Point. At the age of 11, this was my first opportunity to see where he worked and understand why his work clothes got so filthy. As we bounced along on the bus, I remembered one windy, cold, rainy night when Minnie fussed at Porter not to go to work. He was in pain from a toothache that had swollen his jaw to the point his eye was half closed. He wrapped his cap with a scarf to cover his jaw, and off he went into the whistling wind. I cried for him. My father, what a Man!!

Pumpkin Seeds of Thanks

Like Porter loved going to work, no matter the weather or state of health, I loved school. I looked forward to the school bus ride five days a week. Mrs. Fields was my sixth-grade teacher. She was heavy-set with smooth, dark brown skin. Her hair was always in a pageboy with bangs. I enjoyed recess because it was a fun time to talk, run and play with classmates. However, I did so without my friend Flavia, who volunteered to answer the phone in Principal Harris' office during the secretary's lunch hour. She was rarely on the playground during recess. No matter, I was quick to let her know of the goings on.

Other than having a crush on Leroy, who was "too cute" with light skin and curly hair, I have no other recollection of that school year. Regrettably, he rejected me because he liked Delores, who was red bone and pretty, with two very thick, long, black plaits that reached the middle of her back. I was envious of him liking her more than me, but she was a nice girl, whom I thought well of and did not blame her or him for their mutual feelings. I quickly got over it and became good friends with both of them.

Actually, I did not have time for the "who liked whom drama" because about three weeks after school started, Minnie gave birth to Cedric Dean. He was born on a Wednesday in the fall of September 1953. Minnie had been pregnant the year before with a baby girl, but she was stillborn. I had felt Minnie's sadness in losing my baby sister, so when she brought Cedric Dean home, I was thankful that he lived. He looked like a miniature Porter, cute with a long eggy head.

I was delighted my brown-complexioned parents finally had a baby browner than me. He was a powerhouse of energy, crawling, standing and walking by nine months. Being the oldest, I willingly assumed a great deal of responsibility for Cedric's initial care. I did not want him feeling inferior to Jackie and Bay Bay because he was the darkest of us siblings. I never shared my inferiority complex regarding his complexion with him because I did not want to stifle my little brother with unnecessary negatives. During the entire sixth grade, he was my everything. As years passed, I learned my concerns were for naught because Cedric had far greater intelligence, street smarts and confidence in his abilities to succeed than any of us.

***

"Pumpkin Seeds of Thanks" to God for Porter being "a man among men" as well as a loving and hard-working father;

For my delightful bus ride experience with my peers to Bragg Elementary School and the opportunity to see where and how White people lived;

For allowing me to feel puppy love for Leroy, endure rejection, and keep on keeping on;

For my brown-skinned brother, Cedric, whom I loved and could identify with because of the brownness of my skin.

Store Runner

From about 1949 to 1954, I did Village Drug Store and ACME Grocery Store runs for my parents and neighbors for cigarettes, bread, milk and eggs. Neighbors gave me a nickel, dime or, every now and then, a generous quarter (if a little tipsy from whiskey) for each run. I could make 10 to 15 cents on a weekday and up to thirty cents on Saturdays. It was a good hustle, and I loved making my own money. The ACME and Drug Store were closed on Sundays, God's day. When Minnie let me, I used my money to buy Fudgesicles and Orange Creamsicles from the ice cream man's truck on the weekend.

On one of my runs, I stole a five cents Bazooka Bubble Gum in a red, white and blue wrapper from the ACME, not because the devil made me do it, but just to see if I could get away with it. All the way home, I was nervously shaking and looking over my shoulder, expecting any moment the police would grab me from behind and take me to jail. I told God if He let me get away without being caught, I would never steal again. Once home, I hid the gum in the bedroom closet and did not chew it for weeks. When I finally did, it was hard and stale. Thankfully, God gave me a mercy pass and I kept that promise.

Everything was going well until I started running cigarettes and sodas for "Mister," (fictitious name) an older man new to Juniper Lane, the block in back of our house. He was dark-skinned, short, thin, and not too nice-looking with big lips. He lived alone and did not have friends who visited in and out like most neighbors. He either sat at the kitchen window drinking whiskey or on the back steps. From time to time, he would ask me to run for one of the above items. Once getting permission from Minnie, I was off and running. He always gave me a quarter or the change from the dollar. I loved running to the store for "Mister." If sitting on the steps, he would take the item and thank me. If sitting in the kitchen, he would plant a quick wet kiss of thanks on my cheek, which I rubbed off as soon as I walked away.

On one of those kitchen occasions, when I returned from the store with "Mister's" cigarettes, he handed me a dollar, grabbed me to him in a leg lock, and tried to kiss me on my lips. I hollered, pulled away, and hit him until he let me go. He gave me another dollar and told me to keep what happened our little secret. I took that dollar, ran home, and told Minnie. She took me by my hand to his door and confronted him with the rage of a lioness protecting her cub from a predator. Although he called me a liar and denied the incident ever happened, she believed I was telling the truth and left her handprint on his face. The next day she went from backdoor to backdoor, warning the mothers on the block about "Mister." She never told Porter. I did not go near his house again until months later when I joined a gathering of neighbors watching his body being removed by undertakers. No, Minnie did not kill him. Word was he had eaten pork chops and had a stroke.

"Pumpkin Seeds of Thanks" to God for blessing me with a loving and caring mother/daughter relationship that allowed for my revelation of potential harm and Minnie's relentless fierce protection of my well-being.

Uncles

Uncle Son and Uncle Coot were the best uncles ever on Earth. They gave Jackie, Bay Bay, and me everything we needed. Son was born on a Thursday in the spring of 1925. He and Minnie had the same father, Hume Sr., Momma's first husband. Son was six feet and had olive skin, big hands, and a strong build. He was gentle with those with whom he had a relationship but tough as nails when crossed. He took no stuff from anybody, especially the White man calling him "nigger" or "boy." Such ethnic slurs or other racial insults directed at him resulted in physical responses. I recall on several occasions overhearing my parents talk about his hot temper, physicality with a sergeant in the Army, and jaw-breaking fights with those who dared to call him other than Hume (Son) Jackson Jr. He served in the United States Army from 1950 to 1952 as a cook and in the Army Reserve for four years. He looked good in his Army uniform.

When Uncle Son came to visit us on East Cherry Lane, he slept on the couch in the living room, and his feet hung over the arm of the couch. Jackie and I would laugh at his big feet and tickle them to wake him up. Most of the time during weekend visits he would still be tipsy from a hangover from the night before but arose early from bed to cook home fries, grits, eggs, pancakes, fatback, and bacon for breakfast. He could do wonders in that tiny kitchen with just a few pots and pans. He always had a big wad of money. He not only bought the food for breakfast, lunch and dinner, but he also cooked every meal; Minnie loved it, and so did we. That man could cook!

Uncle Son would carry Bay Bay on his shoulders and walk Jackie and me to the ACME Grocery Store and buy all the candy, cookies, and bubble gum we wanted. He kept us spellbound with funny stories about his childhood, growing up in Red Springs with his many cousins. The more he nipped on Kentucky Gentleman, the more exaggerated his stories became. A deep shaking belly laugh would consume him before he concluded the story, and without even knowing the punch line, we would fall out on the floor in uncontrollable laughter, crying and holding our bellies. His natural humor, generosity, and cooking skills brought much happiness to our home.

Preston Drake, my Uncle Coot and Momma's youngest child, was born on a Saturday in the spring of 1929. According to Mamie Doris, Aunt Elma's daughter, Momma was married to a Mr. Crews, but the marriage ended, and she gave Uncle Coot her maiden name.

Uncle Coot was light brown-skinned, short, small-framed, and handsome. He was the exact opposite of Uncle Son, not only in stature, but also in temperament. He was easy-going and tactful; he also had an aura of self-confidence and a spirit of caring that attracted strangers to him. He was an advocate for education and earned a degree from Winston-Salem Teachers College in 1951. I remember him telling us to get as much education as possible because that was the one thing the White man would be unable to take from us. He truly believed obtaining a college degree would not necessarily level the playing field in regards to competing with White folk, but it would position us to seek opportunities in the segregated area of education.

Uncles

Uncle Coot loved himself some Pumpkin, and I loved myself some Uncle Coot. Over the course of various summers, as well as during my stay in Winston-Salem, I was his traveling buddy from Baltimore to Winston-Salem and back. He would twist my greased hair into three short pig tails and dress me in shorts, a blouse, and sandals for our outings to visit his female friends. He showed me off, skinny legs and all. They always made nice over me as his niece. He loved it, and so did I. Considering the number of ladies he visited during any given week, he was a "master player." Uncle Coot had it going on!

Family was everything to both my Uncles Son and Coot. When we suffered hard times due to Porter being on strike for long periods of time from Bethlehem Steel or his gambling losses, they always bailed us out. They were loving, supportive, giving, and very protective of their big sister, Minnie.

I well remember Uncles Son and Coot chipping in together to buy a rollaway bed with a storage cover when we were still on East Cherry Lane. They were probably tired of their feet hanging off the narrow couch when they visited. It reminded me of the rollaway at Momma's house, but the mattress was much larger, and the bed sturdier. As Minnie's family members from North Carolina made frequent visits and were wearing the couch into a lopsided position, the rollaway proved to be the best gift we ever received. Once folded and covered, it fit neatly into a crook of the dining room and became just another piece of furniture.

Pumpkin Seeds of Thanks

☙ • ☞

"Pumpkin Seeds of Thanks" to God for blessing me with two strong-willed, self-confident uncles, who possessed strength, charm, and street sense. Their generosity was unmatched in providing our family love and the necessities of life, especially the rollaway bed, the gift that kept on giving.

Uncles

Uncle Hume (Son)

Uncle Preston (Coot)

Red Top

Porter and Minnie had a gift of hospitality and welcomed many people to our home. They loved family and were sharers. In addition to Uncles Son and Coot, my mother's maternal aunt, Sallie Jane; maternal uncle, David; and her cousins, Della, Currie, Del Tricia, Billy, Ralph, Richard, Daniel, Mamie Doris, Helen, Shirley (Fats), and Barbara Ann, visited often. Those North Carolinians loved visiting us in Turner Station.

Jackie, Bay Bay, and I loved them all, but none of them generated excitement like "too hot to trot" Thelma (Red Top), who had relocated from Red Springs to New York. She was pretty with a red bone complexion, and her dyed red hair was an attention getter. She primped for hours, applying makeup, and dressing in tight short skirts with high heels that accentuated her shapely big legs. She talked fast with constant hand movements, which showed off her long, red, pointed fingernails. Witnessing her laugh was an experience in itself. The more she laughed, the more her upper body would shake, making all of us laugh until tears flowed and our bellies ached. The scent of her perfume was like no other I had smelled. She was gorgeous, our "Miss New York," straight out of the country. Being attractive, curvy as a Coca-Cola bottle, red boned and full of inviting personality, Red Top had it all together.

Red Top enjoyed doing the jitterbug with us, and I showed off my "itch and crouch" moves that I had learned from peeping during parties at Mr. Hus' and Miss Peaches' house. We craved Red Top's attention and tickling as we played on the rollaway during her stay. She put red lipstick on Jackie and me and taught us how to strut and switch our butts in her heels. Much to the irritation of Porter who was not a partier, Red Top's visits attracted men bearing pints or fifths of whiskey like ants attracted to an open syrup bottle. They just wanted to be in her presence and make her happy enough to extend her stay. With Red Top, it was an all-day, half-the-night house party.

Red Top was known for doing pranks, like giving Porter a hot foot when he was asleep on the couch. She would motion for us to be quiet while she put a cigarette between his two bare toes and lit it with a match. Jackie, Bay Bay, and I were not happy seeing her do this because we were afraid Porter's foot might get burned, as well as the couch. He would awake to the heat, jump up, scream, and cuss like the sailor he once was. He would be mad enough to slap Red Top but soon got caught up in her belly-roll laughter and all was forgiven.

During one visit, Red Top talked Porter into letting Minnie go to a party in Baltimore. He was reluctant but gave in after much begging by Red Top. In the wee hours of the morning, we were awakened by the phone ringing, and it was Minnie. I heard Porter hollering and asking several times, "What happened?" Red Top had been stabbed and was in Provident Hospital. Jackie and I cried and held each other all night. Minnie finally came home the next day with lots of dried blood on her clothes. She had Red Top's bloody clothes in a hospital bag and told Porter what had happened. However, they did not share anything with us.

Of course, first chance I got, I peeped into the bag and was scared by seeing all the blood on the sharp outfit Red Top had worn from the house in such high spirit. Based on eavesdropping and peeping, I learned Minnie had tried to stop her bleeding but was unsuccessful. However, the ambulance attendants were able to do so by the time they arrived at the hospital. Also, I learned that the fight occurred because some woman was killer jealous of tipsy Red Top friskily getting down with her boyfriend on the dance floor. I hoped it was not that itch or low crouch move I had shown her.

That night Minnie knelt and prayed with Jackie, Bay Bay, and me at the rollaway bed, asking God to let Red Top live. Minnie hugged and cried all over us. It was the first time we saw her crying, and we all cried too. Thankfully, after a week, Red Top returned to our house, recuperated in our bed, and was restored to not only health but also her fun-loving self. With utter delight, we played and slept on the rollaway for weeks. That rollaway was not only a bed to lay one's head for countless relatives, it was truly a gift that kept on giving, giving and giving.

"Pumpkin Seeds of Thanks" to God for me being aware of His power to answer prayer, for the restoration of Red Top to health, and for her once again being fully able to let the good times roll.

St. Matthew United Methodist Church

St. Matthew United Methodist Church was the Newton family church. I first crossed the threshold of St. Matthew when I was six years old. Dressed in a flower print skirt handmade by Momma, a white blouse, and my Sunday black patent leather shoes with white socks, I was decked out. My hair was in my signature three plaits going every which away. I grinned from ear to ear as Granddaddy introduced me to the heads of the Newton family: Grand Uncle Fred (granddaddy's brother); his wife, Aunt Barbara; Aunt Menyon (my father Porter's sister); older cousins Leonard; his wife, Lenora; Nadine; Ina Clara (Bill); and Horace (Pop). Even more delightful was meeting my cousins, John, Merriel, Maxine, Joan, Michael, and Penny and seeing several of my Day Village friends who belonged to various children's ministries. I was in seventh heaven being with them. The socializing and fellowshipping with family and friends made St. Matthew the place to be.

Every Sunday morning, Pastor John H. Carter talked about God, Jesus and the Holy Ghost. I knew God and Jesus loved everybody and were good, but to my young mind, he preached the same message week after week. Talk about boring. However, when "The Holy Ghost" was mentioned, I was all ears because Momma had deeply scarred me with ghost stories, and my mindset was not to do anything that might result in me tangling with "Him." My goal was to love everybody and be good. The last thing I wanted to do was to upset "The Holy Ghost" and be haunted day and night as I understood ghosts were known to do.

At Momma's Baptist church in North Carolina, I was used to long services with animated preaching, lively gospel singing, people shouting, dancing in the aisle in the Holy Spirit, and the sharing of teary testimonies of God's blessings. The length of the United Methodist services was much shorter but a far cry from the excitement that I experienced in Winston-Salem. The preaching was dry, hymns dragged on for four to five stanzas, choirs were stiff, and the music was uninspiring. The best part was sitting with my cousins, talking and giggling until we were made to be quiet or separated.

I had no singing ability whatsoever, but my Great Aunt Barbara made me join my younger cousins and friends in The Harmonettes Choir. I will forever remember her directing us with her arms waving and fingers pointing as we sang "At the Cross," bellowing out the chorus "At the cross, at the cross where I first saw the light, and the burden of my heart rolled away. It was there by faith I received my sight, and now I am happy all the day." I loved that song and could picture Jesus dying on the cross for me and being both happy and sad about it.

My fondest memory of St. Matthew is when Aunt Menyon took my hand and led 12-year-old reluctant me to the altar for confirmation and baptism by sprinkling. She presented me to Pastor Carter, and he asked the required questions regarding profession of faith to which I replied "yes." I was extremely nervous in front of the congregation, but more so because I wanted to "be right" in doing whatever it was I was doing. I was too scared to play with God and definitely did not want to upset The Holy Ghost.

St. Matthew United Methodist Church

After service, I got plenty hugs and well wishes. Seeing I had made Pastor Carter, Aunt Menyon, and the church members happy, I guessed God must be happy too. I felt an unexplainable warmness in drawing closer to God and really special. I was sorry Porter and Minnie (usher) were not in attendance to witness me accepting Jesus Christ as my personal Savior, being confirmed, and sprinkled. They saw to it that Jackie, Bay Bay, and I attended church regularly because they knew the importance of spiritual nurturing to keep us on the right track, especially that mischievous Bay Bay. Each Sunday, they gave us ten cents apiece for the offering. Without a second thought, I put five cents in the plate and kept five cents to buy penny candy and pretzel rods at the Staple's Store on the way home. That was my Sunday routine.

Annual church picnics to Carr's or Sparrow's Beach, located in Annapolis, Maryland on the shore where the Severn River meets the Chesapeake Bay, were always exciting excursions via school busses. Both beaches were Negro-owned by sisters Mary Florence Carr Sparrow and Elizabeth Carr Smith, respectively, and were two of the most popular beaches in the area open to us. The outings were fun-filled with swimming, fishing, and entertainment. We feasted on fried chicken, potato and macaroni salad, collard greens, string beans, hot dogs, homemade cake, and pies prepared by the cooks of the church. The food was always finger-licking good. St. Matthew was known throughout the surrounding area for the scrumptious dinners, cakes, and pies sold for fundraising.

One year at Carr's Beach, I spotted a line of slot machines and saw a man win lots of quarters from one of them. I ran back to the picnic area and asked my granddaddy, Porter Sr., for change. As usual, he dug into his pants pocket and gave me nickels, dimes, and quarters with no clue it was for playing the slots. As I was not quite tall enough to comfortably reach the handle of the slot machine, I had to jump up, grab it, and pull it down. No sooner than I let the handle go, after a couple pulls, quarters spilled out everywhere. I gathered them up in my blouse and ran back to Granddaddy to show him all my quarters. He was shocked, took me to the side of a building, and in a hushed tone, told me "Baby, if you got caught, you could get in trouble because you are too young to play the gambling machines; church people don't gamble, especially on a church picnic." He took the quarters, put them in a paper bag, and gave them back to me when we arrived at the church. I had 100 quarters! That was the best picnic ever.

Throughout my youthful years attending Sunday School, Methodist Youth Fellowship, Movie Night, Vacation Bible School, and Sunday services, I learned to make wise choices and treat others the way I wanted to be treated. Many of the more senior mother figures were stern and strict. Being sensitive, I shed a few tears resulting from being scolded by Mothers Ollie Cullen, Erma Franklin, Adlee McCullough, Mary Rice, and Margaret Risher. In time, I realized as disciplinarians, they were directing me in the way I needed to go. I eventually came to appreciate and respect their looking out. Mothers Catherine Edwards, Loretha Hancock, Otelia Jones, Anna Mae Mercer, Alice Mondie, and Elizabeth Shelton molded me with gentler correction: caring touch, humorous but common-sense advice, and prayer.

With all the love shown me, I accepted that St. Matthew was the church for me to be. Although the worship music was not stand up, clap, and shout like I experienced during summer vacations with Momma, I adapted to the quiet atmosphere of the services, learned to understand the lyrics of hymns, and tuned into the Word being spoken for the foundation of my spiritual journey and life application.

St. Matthew United Methodist Church

∽ • ∾

"Pumpkin Seeds of Thanks" to God for Pastor Carter, Pastor Sustain R. Bennett, Pastor John R. Brooks, Granddaddy Porter, Grand Uncle Fred, Grand Aunt Barbara, Aunt Menyon, Cousin Lenora, and all those congregants too numerous to name for laying the foundation for my formative spiritual years, especially those who prayed for me before I knew to pray for myself. St. Matthew United Methodist Church was founded in 1900 and, glory to God, continues to be the cornerstone for Christ in the Turner Station community.

Sollers Homes

To my utter surprise and disappointment, we moved to Sollers Homes in the early winter of 1954. Porter and Minnie gave no explanation to my tearful whys and pleadings to stay in Day Village. They just packed us up like thieves in the night, and off we went across the streetcar tracks from bricks to shingles without even a wave, hug or goodbye to my beloved friends on East Cherry Lane.

Of the seven previously mentioned neighborhoods in Turner Station, Sollers Homes was considered to be, by many residents, the least desirable. It was a large community separated by streetcar tracks from Ernest Lyon Homes. Breckinridge Drive, the main street, was the one way in and out. The recreation center located at the entrance was a hub for indoor games and outdoor activities, such as softball, dodge ball, and jump rope. It accommodated the leasing office for one- two- three- and four-bedroom houses as well as rental space by tenants for special occasions and community gatherings.

Breckinridge was bordered by Colfax Way on the right with the Five Fingers swimming area in the rear where the boys often swam in their birthday suits. Burr Way was on the left, parallel to the pond that led to the canal/beach. The Wall (old train trestles) to the left of the beach housed snapping turtles, snakes and several ponds of ducks. Folks from all over Baltimore visited this prime property for swimming, crabbing, carp fishing and relaxation.

Unknown to me at the time, many of the streets of Sollers Homes were named for former vice-presidents of the United States, such as Burr, Tompkins, King, Hamlin, Breckinridge, Colfax, Wheeler, Hendricks, and Fairbanks. Housing in Sollers Homes consisted of modestly constructed one- and two-story shingled and connected dwellings with four to eight families in a block. One-story homes were heated by wood burning pot belly stoves, which were later modernized for kerosene or oil. Wood stoves were used for cooking. Two-story homes were heated via a boiler system, which produced radiator heat that was turned on in mid-October and off in May, regardless of the weather's temperature. Consequently, rent was more affordable than in the other communities. By far, the most significant factor of undesirability was the reputation of Sollers Homes having a disproportionate number of youths labeled as "bad."

I was totally saddened to leave my longtime "good" friends in Day Village to live in Sollers Homes. Initially, we lived at 302 King Court, which was situated in the middle of the community, off of Burr Way. We lived on the second floor with two bedrooms, full kitchen, living room, and bath. Jackie and I quite sisterly shared our bedroom; Bay Bay and Cedric, of course, slept on the prized rollaway.

Apart from the change of neighbors and scenery, our home life remained pretty much the same except that weekend card games became more frequent. In our surrounding area, gambling appeared to be a part of the culture. Neighbors minded their own business and turned a blind eye to what did not concern them. I hated hearing the overnight hushed whispers, betting, shuffling, and slamming of cards in addition to the frequent toilet flushing. I was fearful of the occasional heated accusations of cheating and the possibility of fights. But what upset me most was Minnie having to pass our breakfast plates over the heads of card players, and us awkwardly eating in the living room on Saturday mornings because the card game lasted all night.

After my initial adaptation to my new surroundings, I found people to be welcoming, and a whole new array of playmates, acquaintances, and activities opened up to me. Unlike the one-to three-child families in Day Village, many families in Sollers Homes had anywhere from five to seven children, plus an aunt, uncle, or grandparent living with them. The culture regarding extended families was one of caring, unity, and support: as with the Three Musketeers, "one for all and all for one."

During our 3.5 years on King Court, we had friendly interactions with Sandra and Bo (my age), who lived downstairs. Likewise, we enjoyed frequent good times with nearby neighbors: the Baltimores, Hines, Woods, Pearl (cussing Pearl), Sharon, and her elderly grandfather. Our closest relationships were with the Sherrods (my good friends, Annie and Edna) and the Chambliss family: Mr. Lloyd (dark, tall and thin); his adorable wife, Miss Fannie (light-skinned, plump, cuddly and loving); his sister, Christine (Sis); niece, Anita; and nephews, Johnathan (Bebop) and Donnell.

Mr. Lloyd had one of the few cars in my parent's immediate circle of friends. He possessed the patience of Job, chauffeuring Miss Fannie, Sis, Minnie, and Pearl to Gay and Lombard Street Markets in East Baltimore every Saturday. They would shop for fresh meats, thick slab bacon (my favorite), and other groceries. Shopping for clothes and household items were also part of the experience. As it was a full-day excursion, they always got a pint of Kentucky Gentlemen or I.W. Harper to unwind on the ride back. During those outings, I was responsible for keeping my siblings in check, and I made them mind me with a strap in hand. Bay Bay and Cedric generally obeyed, but Jackie, being the spoiled one, always gave me a hard time until I wacked her legs for being mouthy and not listening. I liked being "in charge."

After one such outing, Minnie had put the food away and was sitting at the dining room table. I put my arms around her shoulders, kissed her, and told her that I thought she should drink whiskey every day. She asked, "Why on earth would you say that?" I told her because she looked prettier, laughed a lot more, and seemed so much happier when she had a nip or two. In my innocence, I actually believed the whiskey was good for her because it loosened her up and she was so much nicer, not constantly fussing. Thankfully, she did not take my advice.

While still on King Court, Minnie gave birth to a preemie, Carole Diane, on a Wednesday in the Winter of February 1956 and brought her home in a hospital cardboard box. She, too, was light-skinned, with everything tiny: head, ears, arms, legs and toes, which Minnie told us not to touch. As she was so fragile, we could look but not hold her. Not even Porter was allowed to do so.

At one month old, precious Carole was lying in the box on the living room couch when Cedric, playing "Mighty Mouse," ran and jumped on top of her. I screamed and tried to pull him out of the box, but he tightly clung to her, as if saving her from some unexpected doom. It was only when Minnie slapped him on the head that he let the crying baby loose. An emergency visit to Dr. William C. Wade determined her to be unharmed. Not quite 2.5 years old, this was the first of Cedric's many playful encounters with his baby sister, whom he adored and protected.

As in Day Village, I was a store runner. I did many runs to the Wilson Grocery Store, which was located near the streetcar tracks at the entrance of Sollers Homes in the rear of a block of one-story houses on Blaine Way. Wilsons was family-owned, as was most

Sollers Homes

of the businesses in Turner Station. It was widely known to have a large variety of groceries, candy and snacks, more so than Hill's Grocery in Earnest Lyon Homes. Although there was no gang affiliation in Sollers Homes, a handful of self- appointed tough males were very protective of the home turf. Due to the territorial attitude of these personalities, my friend Patricia would literally sneak across the tracks with two of her friends to buy goodies from Wilsons. Two of them entered the store, while one served as lookout for the guys who were known to threaten outsiders for daring to venture into Sollers Homes. Thankfully, Patricia and her friends always managed to make it back across the tracks without confrontation.

The rivalry between the two communities was definitely serious. For the most part, those who risked crossing the tracks, even to go to Wilson's store, knew the consequences, if caught. Many potential suitors desiring to visit girls in Sollers Homes dared not walk down the main street; they would cautiously weave their way through side streets, Colfax or Burr Way, in and out of the community with no problems. Where there was a will, there was a way.

More convenient for me than Wilson's was the Foster Grocery Bus. It was located on Breckenridge, centered between Wilsons and the rear of Sollers Homes. The bus provided a shorter distance to buy non-perishable items: candy, snacks, sodas, and cigarettes. At that time, Lucky Strikes, Philip Morris, Camels and Chesterfield cigarettes cost about 24 cents a pack. The corner on which the bus sat stationary was the main hub of peer activity. It served as the hangout spot for everybody "in the know" and was the key lookout point for the Sollers Homes' self-appointed protectors to keep unwanted males out.

I often lost track of time at the bus, chatting with the passersby, namely the Boyd brothers, who swam like fish; the Hintons,

(Mr. Connie, who was dark as coal, handsome, and dapper as a dresser. He was also father of the terror, Leon); the Lewises: James (Slew), who named me "Rock" because he considered me to be a smooth dancer and his brother, Edward, my hand dance contest partner; the McMorrises (Jackie's girlfriends); the Washingtons (Mr. Washington, the dependable transportation hacker); and the Whitbys, (motherland complexions with pearly white teeth, blessed with a quiet, queenly mother). Many a day, Minnie sent Jackie or Bay Bay to tell me to get myself back home with whatever I was sent to pick up. The camaraderie of my peers who hung out at the Foster's bus corner was priceless.

On a cigarette run for Minnie, I was rounding the corner of Hendricks Court (next block over from my street) and was literally ambushed by the Walters family. Although relatively new to the neighborhood from New York, they had a reputation for being rough and tough. From out of nowhere, Dot, who was about my age (14) and five of her brothers and sisters surrounded me with bats and sticks. Nobody else was around. I was scared to the point that my heart felt like it jumped up into my 32A bra and was hiding out among the balls of sweat pouring from me. My entire body was shaking. My mind was racing with thoughts of how to defend myself from the gang beating that was about to go down.

Except for knowing of Dot's older siblings' "going for bad" reputation, I did not know any of them and could not understand why they wanted to fight me. When I stammered that question out of my dry mouth, she replied, "I don't like you because you think you cute." Wow, another crazy fool! Again, that thought never crossed my mind. In vain, I pleaded my case of not thinking I was cute, but to no avail. Dot hit me in the chest, and it was on. Being a couple inches taller, I was able to put her in a chokehold by the collar of her blouse with my left hand, and repeatedly hit on the left side of her face and head with my bony right fist. Terrified, I landed blow after blow only in that one area, while she hit and kicked me. At the same time, her siblings formed a tight circle and beat me with their bats and sticks. All of the above probably happened in less than five minutes, but it seemed like an hour.

Thankfully, a friend of Bay Bay's heard the ruckus and alerted him to my plight; he and his friends came to my rescue. Armed with sticks, they fought and chased away Dot's siblings. I let go of my chokehold on Dot's neck, and she ran home swollen and bleeding. Most of the blows I received from Dot and her siblings were thankfully to my body, no bruises to my face. Looking cautiously over my shoulder, accompanied by Bay Bay and his friends, I continued on my run to get the Lucky Strikes from the Foster Grocery Bus without further problems. As I held the cigarettes in my hand, I thought of the "strikes" I had just received on my beaten body, and I considered myself quite "lucky" to have survived. I was glad not to have been sent for Camels, for, I jokingly thought, I would have had humps and lumps all over me.

Hours later, Dot's mother, Miss Walters, whom we had never met, knocked on the door to tell Minnie I had caused serious damage to her daughter's left ear. Even though Minnie knew Dot initiated the fight, Minnie was empathetic and sorry her daughter suffered ear damage. That is until Dot's mother attempted to give her the doctor's bill. Minnie's face got ugly and turned red. She explained that what had happened was all Dot's fault. Minnie made it clear that I had been minding my own business when her children jumped me, that she would not be paying a "damn" cent, and showed her mother the door.

In time, I held no grudge against Dot, and we became okay with one another. I gained respect from my peers for meeting the challenge of standing up to her, but it was only because I literally had nowhere to run. Bay Bay and his friends continued to play with her brothers and sisters as if the fight never happened, and not once did Minnie hear any more about the payment of the doctor's bill.

Due to frequent breakdowns of the boiler system at King Court and having to use the oven and boiled water to heat the house, we moved to 315 Tomkins Court during the winter of 1957. This apartment had the same configuration as the other one. It was on the second floor with only two bedrooms. The one good thing about the move was that the gambling games were replaced by competitive bid whist, pinochle (rise and fly). I had no clue as to why but was overjoyed for the change. We were fortunate to be blessed with welcoming neighbors: the Commanders, Galloways, Greens, Harrisons, Williamses, and Rouhlacs. They were giving folks who were always willing to lend a cup of sugar/flour or two slices of bread for a mayonnaise sandwich, and likewise expect the same in return when their need arose.

By this time, I not only watched my siblings on Saturdays but I also was responsible for washing and hanging clothes on the line and cleaning the house. We all pitched in except for Jackie. Just as she did on King Court, she would challenge me by saying, "You are not my mother," and I would have to do "the Minnie" on her legs to get her to mind me. By Minnie's return from the all day trip, beds were changed, clothes folded, and the house was spotless. A good report meant I would be permitted to go to Teen Center at Sollers Point High School that night and dance, dance, dance as well as the "Y" on the upcoming Friday night.

Without question, dancing and playing cards were the most popular activities of socialization for the young and the old. In addition, Porter was an avid chess player. He liked most sports, particularly basketball. He taught Bay Bay and Cedric to play chess, but Jackie and I chose to play simple family card games like war, pity pat, go-fish, and spades. I graduated to bid whist and really liked the complexity of the game: bidding for the kitty, big/little jokers, books and points. Porter was a highly skilled card counter and player. He became completely undone and an ungracious loser if I, as his partner (or anyone else), played the wrong card or reneged. After being the receiver of several of his "no, you didn't just play that card," or "what the hell were you thinking" responses, I was turned off completely from playing cards. I chose to watch.

House and spontaneous yard parties within our three-block radius were frequent occurrences and fun, fun, fun. Once the radio or record player in a neighbor's window or on the outdoor steps was turned up, folks came from all over to get down. No food was provided, but in a heartbeat, Minnie or Miss Fannie would prepare fried chicken sandwiches with hot sauce to make a buck. The males seemed to always make a way to put their change together for Boones Farm or Richards Wild Irish Rose wines. Not me, no stimulant was necessary; I was able to let loose to the sounds of Ruth Brown, James Brown, Chubby Checker, Ray Charles, Fats Domino, Little Richard, and Lloyd Price on just the beat alone.

At one of those gatherings, a real unsavory character nicknamed "TT" forcibly gripped me in his arms and, while trying to put his tongue into my mouth, licked me all around my face. I slapped and pushed him away. He became so mad that he threatened to knife me. Thankfully, the tussle was witnessed by two of the toughest guys in Sollers Homes, Lee and Fat Boy, who did not appreciate his man-handling me. They quickly approached us, took him around the corner, and physically addressed the situation on my behalf. He returned with a bloody mouth, muttered an apology, and hightailed it away from the area. I was shaken to the core but got my groove back and danced until Minnie hollered for me to come in the house. In time, I forgave "TT" and became civil towards him, but I never let my guard down in his presence; lesson learned.

As previously mentioned, there were male individuals with a territorial home turf mentality. Their roughneck personalities perpetuated the negative reputation of Sollers Homes among folk unfamiliar with the "caring village nature" of the community. Home turf included the girls living in Sollers Homes. The self-appointed protectors of Sollers Homes confronted all males from across the tracks, the city, or other nearby areas who dared to visit us, homegirls. On occasion, they would fight unwelcomed males at the drop of a hat. Sadly, I witnessed a few boys running back across the tracks to safety, but not all of them made it without knots, bruises, or bloody noses. Retaliation by the injured would occasionally occur at community baseball games or dances. The one terrifying incident I recall was a ruckus at Sollers Point High School during a dance. Guys from Sollers Homes and Earnest Lyon got into a heated dispute, which ended with the firing of a homemade zip gun and utter chaos. Edward (Pi Jo), a respected popular boy from Earnest Lyon, was shot in the back; thankfully, the injury was not life-threatening.

Fortunately, the vast majority of families in this celebrated community were God-fearing, goal setting, and hardworking with offspring who excelled in academics, athleticism, and entrepreneurial skills. Many of the parents were of the "it takes a village mentality." They disciplined, encouraged, and empowered their offspring, as well as neighborhood youth, to focus on achievement no matter the obstacles.

The Baltimore, Bartee, Booth, Boyd, Bradley, Brehon, Brewer, Burrell, Calloway, Cheatham, Cook, Cooper, Covington, Craig, Cromwell, Cullen, Davis, Dent, Dunmore, Ford, Franklin,

Galloway, Haines, Hamilton, Hancock, Harris, Harrison, Heathe, Henry, Hopson, Irby (household of thirteen with parents), Johnson, Jones, Jubilee, Kessler, Koger, Lassiter, Lewis, Lomax, Lynch (large family with celebrity names), Lyons, Orr, Page, Payne, Peaman, People, Poole, Powell, Pryor, Ralston, Reed, Rogers, Rossiter, Saunders, Sharpe, Smith, Sneed, Speaks, Speed, Tate, Turner, Whit, Williams, Wilson, and Wright families are only a few of the many households who positively influenced the "village" of Sollers Homes and will forever remain in the recesses of my mind.

"Pumpkin Seeds of Thanks" to God for the caring and protective village of the Sollers Homes community, the treasure chest of diverse personalities, the spontaneous good times, and the resulting lasting relationships.

Carole (Sister) and Cedric (Brother)

Grand Uncle Dave   **Cedric (Brother)**

Turner Station

In my later teens, I realized moving to Turner Station was the best thing that ever happened to me. It was so much more accessible than being in Winston-Salem, where I was confined to just one block and the park. In this friendly, nurturing community, located less than three miles from the Baltimore City line, I walked in the freedom of movement from home to school and throughout the neighborhoods. Everybody knew one another. I heeded my parents' warnings not to stray beyond the short stretch of Dundalk Avenue. It served as the invisible dividing line between Turner Station and the White communities of Dundalk and Watersedge. Likewise, the streetcar tracks across the street from St. Matthew Church separated us from Old Mill, a small community of White folk.

Actually, there was no need to venture out of Turner Station. It was self-contained with thriving Negro businesses that met every need of the residents. We were blessed with doctors, dentists, nurses, lawyers, teachers, preachers, librarians, hairdressers, barbers, and morticians. Self-innovated entrepreneurs owned grocery stores, five and dimes, gas stations, auto repair shops, laundries, cleaners, printing shops, photography studios, seamstress shops, restaurants, sanitation businesses, trucking companies, and cab services. Electricians, painters, and plumbers (some jack-leg) were visible throughout the community with their trucks and gear. Additionally, a few individual households sold cakes, pies, cookies, penny candies, pretzel rods, or sticky apples. A few popular rock and roll bands and singers were formed in the homes of the band leaders and enjoyed local fame. Everything was within walking distance, including the post office, pool halls, and bars. Earned dollars circulated and re-circulated numerous times.

There were numerous settings for socialization and fun. The YMCA, teen center at Sollers Point High School, Anthony Theatre (owned by Dr. Joseph Thomas), pool halls, and recreational areas (baseball and football fields) were popular venues for gatherings. Swimming, fishing, crabbing, and boating were summer delights. The only White people I saw on a regular basis were the weekly insurance collector, who was, according to Minnie, "put-on friendly" for his benefit, and the milkman.

Turner Station was a safe no-locked doors community. As stated, it was an ideal place to grow up and fulfilled the old African proverb "It takes a village to raise a child." Neighbors cared about each other's children and took an active role in keeping them on the straight and narrow. Men like baseball coach Osceola Smith (Mr. Smitty) and Pierce Jones, Jr. (Mr. Pick); community activists David Barnett and Joseph Butler; and Scoutmaster James Louden trained boys in character building, as did Cubmaster Oliver Riddick; and Cub Scout Den Mother Thelma Louden. Many teachers lived within the area, personally knew our parents, and did not hesitate to let them know the good or the bad. It was indeed a "village."

Occasionally, there were a few incidents where a few rabble-rouser personalities showed out on weekends. These occurrences mainly happened due to indulging in drinking too much wine, which ended in a fistfight or two. However, for the most part, everyone jelled together in peace and harmony. The first Black police officer, James Arthur Johnson Sr. (my buddy, Jimmy's father), was assigned to patrol the area in 1952.

❦ • ❧

"Pumpkin Seeds of Thanks" to God for Turner Station being the segregated mecca of good living and a Christian community where men and women thrived in raising God-fearing and loving families. For placing me in Turner Station at the right time, in the right place, with the right people, allowing me the opportunity to have a testimony of precious lifelong memories and friendships. Praise, Praise, Praise!

Unforgettable Summers

Summers in Winston-Salem, North Carolina, were the best times of my young life. At my asking, Momma allowed me to fill my belly with gingerbread, black licorice candy, watermelon, peaches, snowballs, and root beer pop. With the stretching of daylight, the hot sun darkened my skin beyond Momma's liking. No matter to me, I enjoyed the warmth of the summer heat that allowed me to play outdoors with my friends for hours upon hours. I never tired of the endless games of jacks on the porch, marbles on the dirt, jump rope, dodge ball, and hopscotch on the hot sidewalk. Best of all were the daily trips to the park and dips in the pool until I was barred from doing so.

The cool of sundown was often followed by our creeping about playing hide and seek in between the houses and on neighboring porches. Momma and Miss Phelps, from time to time, got in on the fun by dressing as boogie men or ghosts seeking us out; they were kids at heart. On clear nights, we marveled at the growth of the moon from quarter to full, counted the stars in the sky, teased one another, and giggled for no rhyme or reason, just because our spirits were free to do so. What a time!

All of my summers with Momma were loving and fun-filled. However, my best summer memories, from 1952 to 1959, ran the gamut from being fooled by Momma and Aunt Elma to touring with Momma's gospel choir to frightfully encountering wild pigs to the low point of summer 1955 to making and selling snowballs.

Fooled

"**Fool me once, shame on you. Fool me twice, shame on me.** Fool me three times, shame on both of us" is a quote attributed to Stephen King in his book *On Writing: A Memoir of the Craft*. Agreeably, it's one thing to be fooled one time, but it happened to me not only twice but three times.

On the occasions when Porter hired a friend to drive our family to Winston-Salem for my summer "down-the-country" vacations, we always did a stop in Red Springs, where both Minnie and Porter were born and grew up. It was located a little over two hours from Winston-Salem.

We always visited Porter's family first. His brothers, (my uncles) Kessley, Jessie, Lennis; his sister, Aunt Margie; his sisters-in-law (my aunts) Mamie and Catherine; along with a lot of first cousins would all gather for our arrival at his brother's, Uncle Malien's, and sister-in-law's, Aunt Annie Dora's house. We were served fried chicken, fried corn, corn on the cob, greens, okra, potato salad, homemade biscuits, and Kool-Aid. With full bellies and lots of goodbye kisses and hugs, we traveled about a mile up the road to the house where Momma's sister, Aunt Elma, and her husband, Uncle Wilton, lived. Their children (Minnie's first cousins): Catherine (Cat), Mamie Doris, Helen, Thelma (Red Top), Shirley (Fats), and Joe were always there to greet us.

Unknown to me, Aunt Elma and Momma (Edna) were twins. They were identical in not only skin color, looks, bodyweight and height, but also in the way they talked, walked, sang, laughed; they even had matching handwriting. Both of them were well-versed in Bible scriptures and often quoted them in general conversations among themselves. Momma and Aunt Elma were known throughout Robeson County for their spiritual gift of "talking fire" out of any kind of burn. Momma "talked fire" out of several of my burns but would not share the secret with me or any other family member. All I knew was that while praying over the burn in an unknown tongue, she blew on it and miraculously I was healed as were others.

Momma and Aunt Elma were notorious for standing in for one another and playing practical jokes. I was told that in their younger days, Aunt Elma went to work one day, and Momma the next on the same job; employers never knew they were being deceived. Whenever and wherever they shopped, they bought two of everything to share, be it underwear, dresses, shoes, or coats.

I remember Aunt Elma and Momma tricking me into thinking that they were one and the same. It happened during the summers of 1950 when I was eight and 1951 when I was nine. Upon our arrival in Red Springs, Aunt Elma always pretended to be Momma, and I didn't know the difference. I would run to her for hugs and cuddle in the softness of her stomach, and she would "love on me" like I was her little lost Pumpkin.

After a couple hours of visiting, I would cry uncontrollably as we piled into the car departing for Winston-Salem. Aunt Elma would say, "Don't cry baby, I'll be there when you get there," and she would wave goodbye. Sure, enough as we pulled into the yard in Winston-Salem, Momma would run off the porch to greet me in that same gingerbread smelling dress, and I would once again cuddle in the softness of her stomach. I always asked, "How did you beat us here?" She would reply, "I flew."

Fooled

I fell victim to this foolery until the third occurrence when I was ten years old. I had begun to suspect something was not right the year before, that there were two of them. The light bulb finally came on in that third year when I purposefully set out to determine the truth. I watched Aunt Elma's every move and listened to her offspring refer to her as Momma and Uncle Wilton call her Elma. I knew my Momma only had three children, Minnie, Son and Coot, and her name was Edna. I asked Aunt Elma, the pretend Momma, why she answered to Elma for Uncle Wilton, and why Cat, Mamie, Helen, Red Top, Fats, and Joe called her Momma and him, Daddy. She said Elma was Uncle Wilton's pet name for her, and that she was the children's play mother. I didn't believe that explanation, and could not wait to get to Winston-Salem to further compare my suspicions.

Hot dog! I had left Aunt Elma with gray hair and was welcomed by Momma with black hair. The sham was over when I asked about her hair color and told her my doubts of them being one and the same. She held me to her, confessed and called Aunt Elma on the phone with uncontrollable laughter. The two of them had looked forward to that annual hoax, but I felt shame on Aunt Elma, Momma and all the other co-conspirators who participated in fooling me, especially shame on me.

That was also the first summer Aunt Elma visited Momma's house while I was there. Aunt Elma had come so that she and Momma could rehearse for a big Baptist revival that weekend. They called themselves the Singing Drake Sisters. Except for Momma's dyed black hair, I would not have been able to tell them apart. They looked and acted exactly alike, talking, laughing, singing, dancing and loving on me.

One morning, I overheard them whispering in the bedroom about me, and I later found out why. The two of them set me down on the piano stool in the living room, and gave me the serious "becoming a woman talk." Aunt Elma took the lead asking me if I knew what a "menstrual period" was and what happens when it comes on. I replied "yes." Their next question was "Who told you?" I responded, "My friend, Janet, who was twelve, not only told me but showed me." That was too much information for Aunt Elma. She then turned to red-faced Momma for her follow-up to me, which was, "You can get a baby if a boy touches you. Do not let a boy touch you until you get married. That was the gist of the two-minute talk. I asked no questions but wondered how a boy just touching me could give me a baby. Even at 10, I knew it took more than a touch. Just in playing, many of my friend boys had already touched me. Momma and Aunt Elma were two funny sisters.

***

"Pumpkin Seeds of Thanks" to God for the loving and amusing times I enjoyed with Momma and Aunt Elma; they were truly two peas in a pod, and I cherished the gift of their wisdom and humor.

Grandaunts Elma & Sallie Jane with Momma

Momma's Choir

During the summer of 1953, the Matthew Gospel Singers, a male and female chorus of about 12 singers, rehearsed once a week on Thursday evenings at Momma's house. She was the lead soloist and pianist and could make those piano keys burn with melody. Choir members sang to the glory of God, and sometimes the family pictures fell off the top of the piano. It was not unusual for a member of the group over the course of the rehearsal to cry or shout. My friends and I would sit on the porch or gather in the yard and imitate the soprano and bass singers. We clapped our hands, did the Holy Ghost dance, and pretended to do the "happy" shout. When caught, we were, of course, chastised and told God was going to send us straight to hell for mocking them.

I was "dragged" from church to church on Friday and Saturday nights, never-ending revivals, and all-day services on Sundays. We traveled six to seven persons per car to churches located on remote, country back roads with smelly outhouses littered with torn newspaper on the floor for wiping. I held my bladder for hours because, besides outhouses being dirty, snakes frequented them, and I was terrified of snakes.

I remember telling Momma that I did not want to go to those kinds of churches because I was scared of walking through the field, and the toilets were stinky. She, in plain words, told me not to think too highly of myself because we had a bathroom. She explained to me that God is no respecter of person and that with or without an inside toilet, the choir would sing for any church who invited them because God gave them the talent/gift to sing His Word to everybody; well off or not. I learned a valuable lesson and witnessed many country brothers and sisters give their life to Christ. Even so, I got "happy" when the church had an indoor toilet.

During the services, the choir would set the church on fire with songs associated with celebrated gospel singers. I well remember "How I Got Over," "Surely God Is Able" by the Clara Ward Singers, "Amazing Grace" by the Dixie Hummingbirds, "Move on Up A Little Higher" by Mahalia Jackson, and "Packing Up Getting Ready to Go" by Marion Williams, to name a few.

Mr. Robert Heffner, Momma's husband, whom she married on a Friday in the winter of 1952, always sang one solo, the old Negro spiritual "Go Down Moses." By the time he got to the last refrain, "Let my people go," his face would be wet with tears. That song really moved him, and I wondered if he had been a slave, but dared not ask. I had met him a few years prior and knew they were courting because he came to supper every Sunday and, after eating, always fell asleep snoring on the porch. Even though they seemed to be close, I was surprised she married him because he was deep dark-skinned. They were like day and night; opposites definitely did attract.

To me, Momma and Mr. Heffner were the best singers in the choir. Following Mr. Heffner, Momma always ended the service with her tear-the-house-down Negro spiritual signature song, "Going to Shout All Over God's Heaven." She would begin by playing the piano, sliding from one side of the stool to the other, as the choir swayed to the beat. Then, she would stand up and step out to the floor while another player slid to the stool. As if seeing Jesus in all His glory, with a big grin on her face, she would sing and strut to the beat of the music from the front to midway down the aisle, raise her arms in praise, and act out walking, talking, and shouting all over God's heaven. For the worshippers, it was a foot-stomping, hand-clapping, goose-necking, crying, and in-the-spirit good time. It was my favorite song because once she acted out putting on the robe, crown, and shoes, she had the congregation join in, and they got "fall-out happy." I too was happy because I knew we were at the end of the service and would soon be going home.

***

"Pumpkin Seeds of Thanks" to God, for the primary lessons, I learned from Mama about a "do right life" with God and my witness to her constantly repeating scriptures: do to others as you would have them do to you; what you do in the dark will come to light; you will reap what you sow; give, and it will be given to you; don't judge others; when tempted to follow the crowd, go with the Word of God; and the solid spiritual foundation and inspiration I received in countless churches via the ministry of gospel music performed by Momma, Mr. Heffner, and their gifted choir.

Pig Outing

At about age 12, on a scorching Carolina 100+ degree July afternoon, a couple of my friends and I made the daily trek across the street to the 14th Street Park. It was too hot to swing, seesaw, glide on the sliding board, contort on the monkey bars, or ride the metal merry-go-round. Even though lifeguards were on duty, we were not allowed to go into the massive pool without adult permission, especially non-swimming me. Therefore, we dared not be disobedient and join the swimmers, who were splashing, laughing, and having a frolicking good time playing in the refreshing water.

We soon got bored doing yo-yo tricks and playing jacks in the breezeless pavilion. We refreshed ourselves at the water fountain and decided to cool off in the woods, which was absolutely forbidden by our parents. Nevertheless, we entered the border of the woods adjacent to the park to find shade. The cover from the thicket of trees was cooling as we walked up a hilly incline that surrounded the rear of the park. For a while, we were content running, jumping, laughing, and rough housing with one another.

Once that became humdrum, we attempted to cross a creek by striding two sets of tree logs that connected one side to the other. Being afraid of the continuous moving water, I did not want to walk the logs and risk falling in the creek, but at the others' insistence, I followed and made it safely across, all the time wondering if I could do the same on the return. We threw rocks into the creek and woods beyond while laughing and clowning about the boogeyman. When suddenly we heard sounds of pigs squealing and snorting; we had intruded into dangerous wild pig territory. Within seconds, a dreadful-looking, overweight, dirty brown pig with huge nostrils appeared through the shadowy trees. There was no time to holler "Lord, help!;" he was looking straight at us.

It was truly a time of "me, myself and I." With ballooned eyes, a fast-beating heart, and marathon legs, I high-tailed it to the crossing just as that monstrous pig and another came out in pursuit. I crossed those tree logs running like the Olympian track star Jesse Owens. I ran for my life without ever looking over my shoulder for the others until I made it back to the border of the park. Only then did I realize that the wild beasts were no longer pursuing us. Shaking and crying, I fell to my knees, gasping for breath. Hearing the chatter and laughter of the swimmers in the nearby pool was music to my ears. Except for a few scratches from tree branches, we were all unharmed.

After that, my friends and I no longer found the park to be boring in 100+ degree heat and never did the pig run again. I did not tell Momma, and neither did the others tell their parents of our near-death experience.

༺ ● ༻

"Pumpkin Seeds of Thanks" to God for allowing me to survive the pursuit of the wild pigs and learn a lifelong lesson from the consequences of disobedience.

Summer of 1955

I was bursting with excitement the day after school closed that June knowing I would soon be home with Momma. Porter and Minnie loaded us up in Mr. Commander's Cadillac at 5:00 AM to make the trip to Winston-Salem via Route 301. Mr. Joe was Porter's friend, a tall, heavyset, dark-skinned man, who was a neat dresser and a nice man who loved driving. They and Minnie sat in the front seat while Jackie, Bay Bay, Cedric and I sat tightly in the back. On the floor between our legs were three shoeboxes filled with fried chicken, a loaf of white bread, and pound cake. The trip was fun. We played tic-tac-toe, read comic books, ate fried chicken with cake, and fought over a space to sleep. We were not allowed to drink water from the canning jars or bottled soda to avoid needing bathroom breaks before getting to gas stations that served Negroes. If one of us could not hold his or her bladder, Mr. Commander pulled off to the side of the highway for a quick pee. Minnie shielded Jackie's and my squats with the open back car door while we peed in the grass. My brothers were also shielded, but it took much less effort for them to relieve themselves.

After many chants of "How much longer?," we would arrive and see Momma sitting on the front porch. Once Mr. Commander parked the car in the yard, she and all the neighbors in the apartment building would run out to the car to greet us. It was a happy moment of hugging and kissing. We kids stayed with Momma while Porter, Minnie, and Mr. Commander stayed with nearby cousins.

Pumpkin Seeds of Thanks

Once we kids ate, we were eager to go to the pool across the street in the 14th Street Park. We always had to wait one hour because we had been told time and time again, "If you swim right after eating, you will get a cramp and drown." Not that any of us could swim, but we loved to play in the shallow section of the water and always obeyed the lifeguard's instructions. We had big fun in the park and pool during that long weekend visit. Hugging and saying goodbye to my parents and siblings at their departure back to Baltimore was tearful. However, Momma comforted me by letting me join my friends in the pool. The water was so refreshing in that hot and muggy North Carolina heat.

Later that night, Momma received the expected "collect ploy call" whereby Minnie deviously asked to speak to herself to let Momma know they were home and all was well. However, this was not the case. Bay Bay was sick. He had experienced a headache, fever, numbness, and loss of muscle function in his legs during the trip back home. He could barely walk.

At the time, polio was a terrifying epidemic among children. Minnie knew the symptoms, and she attributed his condition to frequenting the public swimming pool that weekend. At that time, community pools were associated with being the perfect breeding ground to become infected with it. She told Momma to check me out. I was perfectly fine, but Minnie barred me from the pool for the rest of the summer, and I readily obeyed. I knew about polio and had seen children on television with the disease wearing braces and lying in iron lungs, the machine for breathing. I did not want my little eight-year-old brother to be crippled, wear braces, or live in an iron lung. Momma and I prayed.

Per Bay Bay, on his initial visit to Dr. Harold Nichols' office in Earnest Lyon Homes, even with leaning his body weight on Minnie, he struggled to walk. He whined and coughed continuously as he

Summer of 1955

limped across the grassy field, which was a short cut between Day Village and Earnest Lyons Homes. He was terrified the doctor would tell Minnie that he was dying and begged her to take him back home. Minnie set him down, slapped him, gripped him by the shoulders, looked him in his eyes, and told him that he had to "fight" to get better.

As Minnie feared, Bay Bay was diagnosed with polio, the common name for poliomyelitis, inflammation of the spinal cord. It was a contagious disease thought to be spread through contact between people through nasal and oral secretions in the mouth. After several visits to City and University Hospitals with no improvement in his condition, he was given a spinal treatment at Johns Hopkins Hospital. In a three-month period, he fully recovered with no residuals.

Between the ages of nine and 10, Bay Bay learned to swim like a fish at the two local Turner Station swimming sites off of Bear Creek: Five Fingers in Sollers Homes and the Trestle in Earnest Lyon Homes, where the males swam in their birthday suits. He was fearless when swimming in any water, ocean or pool. He once cured himself of poison ivy by swimming for long periods of time in the water at Five Fingers. As a result of Bay Bay's bout with polio, I remained fearful of water and never learned to swim like Jackie and Cedric. Minnie's "slap of encouragement" toughened Bay Bay to fight to walk; he never looked back. As a teen, he could almost out dance me, the "Rock."

The summer of 1955 was also the year I lost my big toenail on my right foot. Cousin Weldon drove Momma and me way out in the country to a farm to buy live chickens, vegetables, and cured hams. While they were transacting the sale with Mr. Tim, the farmer, I, without permission, ventured into the stable to see the horses. All was well until I quietly stepped to the back of one horse to pet and talk to him. Unlike in the movie *Francis the Talking Mule*, this horse was not friendly. He started snorting and squealing, raised his leg and stomped hard on my size 5 foot. As if that were not enough defense of his space against my invasion, he kicked the front lower part of my leg above the ankle and I bled instantly. I was scared to death that he was going to trap me in the stall and kill me.

Thankfully, a farmhand came to my rescue and got me out of the stable. The pain was toe-curling. As I cried uncontrollably, the man carried me over to Momma, who looked terrified as we approached her. She had no clue I had wandered off on my own. After she poured some alcohol on my leg and toe, Cousin Weldon carried me to the truck to wait their completion of the sale. The time seemed forever, and I cried worse than I had ever seen Jackie cry. Over the course of about two weeks, my nail turned black and fell off totally. After the rawness healed, I kept red nail polish on the hard skin to camouflage not having a nail. It grew back after a couple of years, but my right big toe never regained its natural contour and remains flatter than my left one. The wound on my leg took years to heal, and I still have the mark from that dreadful day.

◈ • ◈

"*Pumpkin Seeds of Thanks*" to God for not only healing Bay Bay of polio but also for blessing him to be a loving, generous -to-a-fault brother who became an excellent swimmer and smooth dancer.

For God's healing of my toe and wound, restoration of my nail, and Momma's nursing skills in caring for me throughout the entire painful ordeal that summer.

Doo-doo Sandwich

The Bay Bay/polio drama was not the only memorable event during the summer of 1955. For the first time ever, I found myself in "sho'nuff" deep trouble with Momma. I willingly participated in a cruel prank on Isaiah, one of my playmates, who lived a few blocks from me in the area of Miss Mamie's neighborhood. He was a "tattletale" and beggar, always begging for whatever he saw, whether it be candy, cookies, fat back and jelly sandwich, biscuit or cornbread. If he saw it, he asked for a piece or bite. "Gimme, gimme" were always the first words from his mouth. If we did not give to him, he would threaten to tell whatever mischievous act he had been privy to see or hear us do. He constantly begged for any and everything.

One day a group of us were talking about Isaiah being a pest and getting on our nerves. Someone suggested we trick him by making a pork pudding sandwich mixed with a little doo-doo in the middle and pretend it was yummy. After a couple days of storing our breakfast pork pudding, we had enough to carry out our sick plan. We removed the casing from the pork pudding, generously spread it on the jellied bread, and placed the turd in the middle of the sandwich.

Seeing Isaiah approaching, we began acting like our pudding and jelly sandwiches were lip-smacking good. Sure enough, he fell for the setup and begged, "Gimme, gimme." To his surprise and delight, we gave him a whole sandwich. He obviously did not smell it or taste it with the first bite, but as he took the next bigger bite, he tasted the doo-doo. With disbelief in his bulging eyes, he immediately spit it out of his mouth and ran home gagging, puking, crying, and hollering to the top of his lungs. That reaction was a shocking surprise. We had expected Isaiah to spit it out, laugh, and forget about it as a good joke, maybe be a little upset but not run home. What were we thinking? This was tattletale Isaiah.

We knew we had gone too far and were in deep trouble and that our little prank would soon come back on us big time. Later that evening the doo-doo hit the fan. It all came to a head when I spotted Isaiah's parents, with stern frowns on their faces, walking toward our apartment building with him sheepishly lingering behind them. My heart beat so fast that I had to hold my heart to keep it from jumping out of my body. I was shaking scared. They told Momma what had happened, and all three adults concluded that God did not like evil and I was going straight to hell if I ever did anything like that again. Momma was so shocked and disappointed in my behavior that she threatened to make me eat a doo-doo sandwich, too. I remember thinking whose stinky doo-doo would it be, hers or mine.

I was made to apologize to Isaiah and beaten by Momma for the first time ever with a leather strap. With at least ten lashes, she repeated, "Don't ever do that again" and gave me a week of in-house punishment. Upon being allowed out to play, I saw Isaiah sitting across the street in the park pavilion with the other playmates who had participated in the prank. He was waiting to play with me as if nothing had happened. All was well. From then on, when Isaiah said, "Gimme, gimme," he only had to ask me once. I loved that boy, and he loved me. In case you are wondering, I truly do not recall whose doo-doo it was, but it was not mine.

ಳು ● ಳು

"Pumpkin Seeds of Thanks" to God for this teachable moment to do to others as I would have them do to me, for His merciful pardoning, and for Isaiah being such a forgiving soul.

Snowballs

Momma could make a dollar one way or the other. She sewed/altered clothes and sold pies, cakes, gingerbread, and finger-licking good chicken dinners. But her biggest moneymaker was her snowball stand. As mentioned previously, our house was located directly across the street from the 14th Street Park, which provided recreational activities and a huge swimming pool for Negroes. Busloads of kids visited on weekends in the summer from not only Winston-Salem but also Greensboro and High Point, North Carolina. Our close proximity to the park was the perfect location for Momma to sell snowballs, pop, candy, and gingerbread. When the busses rolled in, we were ready; Momma made money.

Between the summers of 1956 and 1959, when I was ages 14 through 17, Momma worked me like a Motherland slave, selling snowballs during the week, more so on the weekends. With an ice block hand shaver and flavored syrups, ranging from cherry and grape to orange and egg custard, I quickly became an expert in making tasty snowballs at record pace. I worked with Momma, shaving the ice, filling the cups, adding the flavorings, and collecting the five cents. This was a "for sure moneymaking business."

I enjoyed serving the long lines of kids, especially the cute boys. When Momma saw a boy grinning at me, she would hurry them along, especially the darker ones. The exception was Carl, who was light-skinned, cute, always neatly dressed, and mannerly. With both of his parents being teachers, he more than met Momma's criteria of a worthy friend for me. Although he lived about 12 blocks away, he came to buy snowballs at least once a day and was warmly welcomed by Momma. On weekends during the peak of the selling frenzy, he hung around to carry ice and gallon jugs of syrup from the kitchen, even pitching in to shave the ice when things got hectic. Our hands would touch, and we would be all gums, grinning like two Cheshire cats. We never kissed, but being in his presence made the summer of 1956 as sweet as my favorite coconut custard snowball.

Momma was a smart entrepreneur and always got the most of her dollars. Her trick of the trade was adding five-cent packs of sugared Kool-Aid with one and a half quarts of water to the expensive half-gallon flavored syrup. As it was a secret between us she did the mixing in the kitchen at night with the shades drawn and door closed. She immediately burned the empty Kool-Aid packages in the wood stove. In the event that health inspectors popped in, as they did occasionally, the flavored syrups were already mixed with the Kool-Aid in the original brand tightened bottles. I worried about her getting caught, but she was a master mixologist when it came to stretching snowball dollars. We were known for miles throughout and beyond the 14th Street corridor for making the tastiest snowballs, and we enjoyed very profitable summers.

"Pumpkin Seeds of Thanks" to God for the hard work ethic I learned from Momma, who often quoted II Thessalonians 3:10-12, which states, in a nut shell, no work, no food. I was taught as a youth to put forth my best effort in all my undertakings.

Rocking Through Challenges

As I stated in the preface, many of my experiences are written in life chapters, overlapping my stays between Winston-Salem and Turner Station. This final chapter, "Rocking Through The Challenges," highlights the good times, not-so-good times, twists, and turns of my encounters while a student at Sollers Point Junior-Senior High School from September 1954 through June 1960.

In the summer of September 1954, I returned home from Winston-Salem with my suitcase full of newly-bought department store clothes, shoes, and school supplies to begin my first year at Sollers Point Junior-Senior High School. Being 12 and entering seventh grade, I no longer wanted to wear the handsewn clothes Momma made me from decorative cotton seed sacks. My Uncle Coot had treated me to a shopping spree, and I was happy and excited. As always, Momma had sent me off with a prayer to God for her Pumpkin to shine among the other students and for me to make her proud. I knew if she could talk the fire out of a burn, as previously mentioned, I was good to go.

On my first day with much apprehension, I entered the doors of this massive brick building in awe. The principal's office was on the right and housed Mr. Charles W. Fletcher, principal; Miss Elizabeth S. Williams, vice-principal; and staff members

Miss Brown, Mrs. Jenkins, and Mrs. Randall (sweet mother of classmate Julia in first grade). Steps leading to the auditorium and gym were across the hall on the left. I was amazed at what appeared to be an endless range of classrooms on both sides of the long-polished hallway. It was so clean. There were several sets of stairs leading to more rooms on the second floor. The width and length of the building... were overwhelming.

I was very much aware of the outstanding reputation of Mr. Fletcher, Miss Williams, and the other teachers, many of whom lived in the neighborhoods and interacted with parents on a daily basis. They were known to be knowledgeable in their subject matter and highly professional in their teaching abilities; they were disciplinarians and role models of success.

Sollers Point was built in 1948 and, in just six short years, was recognized as a respected institution of higher learning and athletic success in track and field among other Negro schools. Former students boasted of the excellent academic preparation they had received, which made them competitive in seeking higher education and employment. I knew this experience would not be a cake walk, but I was ready to put my best foot forward.

Mr. Leonard L. Saunders was my homeroom teacher. He taught mathematics to all seventh and eighth graders. Handsome, well-dressed, and well-groomed, he could have been featured on the cover of Ebony Magazine. A banner, "Mathematics Is the Science of Numbers," hung above the blackboard. He lived and breathed mathematics, and the motto was drilled into our minds by reciting it every day at the beginning of class. He was an excellent teacher, but regrettably I did not have the math gene of my paternal great-grandfather, Raeford Newton, who in the late 1800s was known as "the Mathematician" of Red Springs. Likewise, my father, Porter; my brothers, Bay Bay and Cedric; and many of my male cousins excelled in math. My only desire was to pass the class, but because of Mr. Saunders' ability to teach, I exceeded my own expectations.

I loved everything about Sollers Point: changing of classes, teachers, lunch in the cafeteria, extra-curricular activities, and socialization before, during, and after school. Once the bell rang for dismissal, I was out the door for a few quick dances to the jukebox at Ransom's Restaurant, a half block away. I stayed there no more than a half hour to avoid punishment for not coming straight home. Nothing was worth not being able to go to the weekend dances. On the rare occasions when Minnie kept me home from school because of a cold or flu, I was sicker from missing school and my socializing than from being sick. I cried and pouted all day. School was my everything and then some.

Although I had no artistic ability, I looked forward to classes with Mrs. Lucille Venture, the artsy Art teacher. She dressed in bright-colored combinations long before color boldness became fashionable and wore big jewelry accessories, a memorable character. I did not do too badly with the multi-colored pencil art but was messy with paint projects. My favorite drawing was a house with a chimney, two windows, door, flowers, grass, one tall tree, and a powder blue sky with fluffy cumulus clouds, highlighting the sun in the background. It was my vision of a dream family home.

Miss F. McMillan, my science teacher with the signature long bangs and stylish page boy hairdo, was a walking encyclopedia of scientific laws and theories based on cells and molecules. Her wealth of knowledge was amazing to me. I liked her.

In eighth grade, I was taught Core (English, social studies, literature) by Mrs. D. Atkins, with whom I also had homeroom.

Pumpkin Seeds of Thanks

Physical education with Miss Lovie Williams was fun, but I hated wearing the gym suit showing my skinny legs and taking showers with the big breasted and fat butt girls. Music with Mrs. Clara Green in the eighth grade as well as in senior high was challenging. I had no singing ability or musical inclination whatsoever. She worked hard with me to develop my voice in the right key to no avail. No amount of musical scales and interval exercises ever helped; singing was not my gift. However, it was interesting to learn music theory: how a song was composed with notes, scales, chords, timing, beats and rhythm. Even so, as an avid listener of and dancer to rock and roll music, structure of a song was of no interest to me, only the words, a good beat, and rhythm. I could sing along to those songs all day long, on or off key. Even though I never developed any musical ability, Mrs. Green showed a soft spot for me, and we shared a warm fondness for one another.

By the end of eighth grade, that cute, curly-haired Leroy, on whom I had a crush in the sixth grade asked me to be his girlfriend. I no longer was interested in him. I rejected his request as being too little, too late. He was not a happy camper.

That rejection of Leroy was due to my attention being caught up with my infatuation with Baldy, who was tall, dark as a rock of coal, and handsome, with a killer smile of pearly white teeth. He was a thinker, not a dancer. We spent fun times together in and out of each other's homes playing checkers, dominoes, cards, and Monopoly. We sat on my steps and flipped pages in Ebony magazines for hours, talking about entertainers, movie stars, and seeing the world. I was saddened when his family moved to the city, but we maintained our friendship for several years with visits and calls until we lost contact.

In ninth grade, I had Mrs. Louise Lamb, a caring and encouraging teacher, for homeroom and Core. Rather than teaching just through books and lectures, she taught how to use the gift of senses to touch and feel people, places, and things.

We took a class trip to the United States Capitol Dome and Rotunda in Washington, D.C. for our final grade and were instructed to write a paper on the visit. Other than going to North Carolina and seeing the boring route of endless trees, tobacco, and cotton farms on Highway 301, I had not been exposed to travel. So, riding the bus into the heart of D.C. to tour the Capitol afforded me the opportunity to see the hustle and bustle of working people and fellow tourists, as well as the impressive architecture of the building itself. During the tour, my classmates were busily taking notes while I took in the length, breath, and height of the massive openness of the building. I was truly big-eyed by the magnificence of the ceiling paintings, color, art, marble, and the detail of the life-like statues. I took no notes.

One week later, true to form, last-minute me sat at the kitchen table from 8:00 PM until midnight, handwriting and rewriting my paper, which was due the next day. The following week, Mrs. Lamb passed out all the graded papers except for mine. I thought, "Uh oh, was it that bad that she trashed it?" She then gave some glowing remarks about the A+ paper she was about to read to the class. As she began reading, I realized it was my paper. I was flabbergasted to receive such high approval and showed my wide, crooked, big-toothed smile the rest of the day.

Another memorable moment in ninth grade was an encounter I had with Ollie, who, in my opinion, was the handsomest boy in the entire school. God made everything about him fine, fine, fine: striking good looks, olive brown complexion, well-molded body, and an inviting smile with a gentleman's personality. Since entering seventh grade, I had been in awe of him from a distance, not romantically but because he was just so fine to look at.

One day while in the hall on a pass to go to the restroom, I saw Ollie approaching me from about four classrooms away. It was just us; my heart beat the fast rhythm of a jamming African drummer. I was thrilled to see him stepping toward me with a charming grin. As God would have it, I was dressed in the finest outfit I had ever owned in all my nine years of schooling: an off-white wool blend skirt and olive green long sleeve knit top (given to me by my second cousin Ina Clara, who lived in New York and wore expensive clothing). He smiled broadly and said, "Hello, wow, you are cute as a bug in that outfit."

If I had been a Hershey bar, the chocolate would have melted all over that off-white skirt. From then on, even though he was a senior three years older than me, he always acknowledged my presence no matter where or who he was with. I cherished that one just-by-chance compliment and continued kindness. I wore that outfit on a weekly basis for the remainder of the winter season until the skirt faded from off-white to a dingy beige.

During that time, Clarence and Pete (brother of the terror Leon from fifth grade) were swarming like honey bees competing for me. Both were dark-skinned, good-looking, and about the same in height; however, they differed in personality. Clarence was soft spoken and easy going. Pete was rough around the edges. He cussed like a sailor and, like Leon, would fight without hesitancy, but he had a generous, loving spirit. Pete lived near the hang-out spot by the Foster Grocery Bus, which was located midway Sollers Homes, and Clarence lived in the rear. Although they were not the greatest dancers, I liked them both and enjoyed our long talks but never entered into anything more than a friendship with either of them.

Without question, my first heartthrob at 14 was Gary. He was a cutie: beautiful olive complexion; curly hair; short, small frame;

sharp dresser; and smooth dancer. Because he lived in Earnest Lyon Homes, he traveled the back roads to visit me. He was just super nice, not a fighter. Our courtship consisted of holding hands as we walked together as well as, dancing at the YMCA and the Sollers Point Teen Center, ending with a good-night peck on the cheek.

One day Gary dropped by unexpectedly and caught me in shorts, and I was visibly embarrassed for him to see my bulging knees on my bony legs. Regrettably, my legs were identical to those of my father, Porter, and other Newton relatives. I never understood how with me being a girl, I did not get Minnie's pretty shapely legs. Gary put my concerns to rest when he assured me with the seriousness of a heart attack that my legs complimented my 92-pound body. Even more so, he complimented me for having nice thighs. For sure, I wore shorts from then on.

We jelled well together for about a year. That is until my heart was crushed when Gary dumped me for Maureen with no warning other than a call to say "I quit you" and hung up. Although puzzled, I thought nothing of it. We had quit each other before for one silly reason or another but not meaning it for more than a few hours or a couple of days. Knowing I had not given him any cause to break up, I dismissed it as unfounded "whatever."

At the Sollers Point Teen Center that night, Gary was cordial but aloof with me. He kept dancing with Maureen, who was cute and bow legged. With her white bobby socks rolled down to her ankles, her curvy legs were even more noticeable. When time came to walk me home, I glimpsed him escorting her out the door and wondered what in the heck had just happened. I had no clue. As all eyes were on me, I could have earned an Academy Award for pretending I was cool while hurting to the depth of my soul. I skipped my usual drop-in at Ransom's Restaurant. I had no desire to hang out and get a few more dances from the jukebox with Moses, Slew, and Ed, my favorite hand dance partners. I teared up as I ran across the shadowy, dark field to the comfort of home. It was a devastating blow to experience at my tender young age, but I survived and was able to say "no" when he came crawling back a few months later, asking for a second chance. I forgave him for that teenage heartbreak but had no desire to ever be with him again.

Shortly thereafter, at 15, I had a liking for Carroll (Foball). He was dark brown and attractive and had a warm smile. Wow, he could sing. It was only for a fleeting moment that we talked because when it came to decision-making time between me and Annie Mae, who was also vying for him, he chose her. However, unlike Gary, he was straight up, informing me that he cared for me, but his affection for her outweighed his fondness for me. I respected his frankness and enjoyed a chummy friendship with him until he joined the Army. I considered him to be a caring friend.

Tenth grade was curriculum decision time: academics... commercial or general. As I had no funds to attend college; no wish to learn French, travel to France, or be taught mathematics by Mr. Arthur Morton (whom I academically feared); and no desire to learn typing and clerical skills to become a secretary or enter the business world, I chose general. I planned to make it out the door with a diploma in hand, join the United States Marine Corps Women's Reserve, travel the world, interact with people of all nationalities, and later pay for college via Uncle Sam's G.I. Bill.

Both Momma and Minnie were opposed to my career choice of becoming a Marine. They were of the opinion, per hearsay, that take-charge, bulldagger women in the armed service would convert naïve me into being one. At the time I was only familiar with two terms: "funny," meaning not acting in the gender born, and "sissy," boy acting like a girl. I only knew one guy in the entire Turner Station community who talked girlishly, switched, and was referred to by some as "a sissy." He was a "lovable character," liked by me, most of the school body, and most residents of Turner Station. As I had never encountered any "funny" girls, I considered their concern for me as unfounded.

History with Mr. Joseph Woolfolk was a delight in that he was able to make boring past events come to life with his knowledge of historic occurrences and humor. His relationship with students was professional as a teacher but, to most students, inviting as a friend.

I was thrilled to be in home economics with Miss C. Johnson for cooking and sewing. Unlike with Momma's and Minnie's freehand meals and baking, everything in class was precisely measured. Likewise, with sewing, I learned by patterns and concentration. I was used to seeing Momma's fast, free hand cutting of feed sack material for my skirts and hearing the fast hum of the Singer sewing machine as she switched the material from one side to the other with fast jerky movements, all the while telling me to do this or that. Momma was competently self-trained.

The only class I disliked in the general curriculum was biology. Dissecting mice in Mrs. Gladys Saunders' biology class was really stressful. I was terrified of mice and felt particularly heartless cutting on the lifeless bodies of the little critters. I would flashback to my perception of Momma cruelly killing the helpless chickens.

All was going super well for me in the tenth grade; I was happy! That is, until the morning of Saturday, March 8, 1958, when my very being was introduced to the darkest day of my almost 16 years.

Pumpkin Seeds of Thanks

A Western Union telegram was delivered to our door addressed to Minnie. It read "Preston Drake killed in car accident." It was from Momma. Minnie screamed and fell to her knees. As on cue, I, too, screamed and fell to my knees, crying uncontrollably, "not my Uncle Coot."

Porter attempted to comfort us, but he too broke down, and each one of us was on our own to deal with that shocking news. Then all of a sudden, Minnie wondered aloud if the telegram was referring to her brother Uncle Coot or her first cousin Preston Drake, for whom Uncle Coot was named. As our phone was out of order, she and Porter took off running about a half mile to Uncle Jimmy's and Aunt Menyon's house in Ernest Lyon Homes to call Momma. Jackie, Bay, Cedric, Carol and I kneeled and prayed along the cushions of the couch for it not to be Uncle Coot. I really liked cousin Preston, and I did not want him to be dead, but Uncle Coot was my loving doting uncle who was my everything: my heart. What a dilemma!

Porter and Minnie returned with him holding her closely, and no words were necessary. Her look of disbelief and swollen eyes spoke the words she could not say and that we were dreading hearing. Uncle Coot was dead!

According to the police on the scene, Uncle Coot had apparently fallen asleep at the steering wheel on Highway 150 on Route 3 in route to Momma's home. The car ran off the road and flipped over; his chest was crushed, killing him instantly. We learned from Uncle Coot's co-workers that he was extremely tired that evening from teaching and working long hours, as well as tutoring that week. He did not heed their requests to rest before getting on the road, and his refusal to do so resulted in untold misery for so many, especially Momma, Minnie, Son, and me. For me, there would be no more calls, visits, hugs, kisses, "just us" trips from

Rocking Through Challenges

Turner Station to Winston-Salem and returns, no more mailing him my hand-copied report card and no more right from wrong talks. He had promised me a weekend at the Atlantic Beach in South Carolina as a sixteenth birthday gift that coming summer. I selfishly blamed God for letting Uncle Coot die but more so Uncle Coot himself for not listening to his co-workers' advice to rest before getting on the road. This one moment in time left me heartbroken, confused, and mad.

To my surprise, I was not allowed to go with Minnie to the funeral. Momma feared that seeing my adored Uncle Coot laid out in a casket, looking asleep but unable to wake up, would be too traumatic for me. She had never forgiven herself for my harrowing experience with the "casket lady" and did not want to cause me further digression with my stammering. I was so pained.

Minnie's friend cussing Pearl traveled by Greyhound with Minnie to the funeral. At Minnie's pleading, Pearl did not say one cuss word during their entire week's stay in Winston-Salem. Pearl's heartfelt love for Minnie and respect for the elders allowed her to control her cussing habit. Momma and Aunt Elma were very appreciative of Pearl being such a special friend. Pearl scored a lot of brownie points with the family. Being frugal themselves, they could not get over the fact that Pearl used her own money to ride the bus from Baltimore with Minnie to Uncle Coot's funeral and contributed to buying whatever was needed for the house.

Minnie's play by play of all that happened at the funeral made me cry and laugh. The funeral was attended by all the Drake family, but me, plus a standing room crowd of other mourners: fellow college grads, throngs of students whom Uncle Coot had taught, faculty with whom he had worked, friends, neighbors, and even White people. Minnie humorously shared that 50 percent of the funeral-goers were "fall out crying" women who thought they were "the one." A couple of his main squeezes passed out upon entering the church; several of them kissed him in the casket, and one had to be held back from falling in the grave. She said that with all the "walk on water" praises piled on Uncle Coot by the preacher, she knew he had gone straight to heaven to be with Jesus Christ and would forever be my guardian Uncle angel. I believed her.

Around my sixteenth birthday, Mert, my friend since first grade, introduced me by telephone to Sylvester, his childhood friend and neighbor. Sylvester was looking for girls to come to a spur-of-the moment party. George and Sylvester were throwing the get-together at his brother Carroll's (Bubbles's) and sister-in-law Ruth's house in Day Village (unknown to them). George was Ruth's brother and was entrusted to babysit their children, Carroll, Jr. and Janice. I later learned that Bubbles' band, "The Imperials," was widely known all over Baltimore and played on weekends throughout the city. George and Sylvester had frequent unauthorized parties while George babysat.

I knew Minnie would not permit me to go, but I strung Mert along as if I was coming. I called him back every 20 minutes to see who was there and what was happening. Well, on my fourth call, Sylvester took the phone from Mert and said, "Look girl, if you are coming, come; if not, stop tying up the phone asking questions" and hung up. I figured Sylvester suspected after my third call that I had no intention of coming to the party. I chuckled and wondered who in the world that rude guy was and forgot about it.

Apparently, curiosity killed the cat because the next day, Mert called and asked could he bring Sylvester over to meet me and I was agreeable. Sylvester had no problem coming into Sollers Homes because he had a close relationship with George (the party-giver), who was well-known for his ability to hold his own in a fistfight and talk his way out of anything. Likewise, his friend Lee, who was one of the toughest boys in the community, gave Sylvester free rein in and out.

Once we shared the pleasantries of introduction, I sized Sylvester up as considering himself to be an East Baltimore slick ladies' man. He was pleasingly good-looking with full lips, poppy brown eyes, and a reddish dark brown complexion. He had close cut hair. He was small-framed and short in stature but a giant in confidence with a distinct swag. The boy looked good: neatly dressed in a hat, starched shirt, khaki pants, and Stacey Adams shoes.

After about an hour of small talk, Sylvester became bored and got up to leave. I do not know why, but I stuck my foot out to stop him, and he tripped. Then things got a little uncomfortable. He tried to kiss me, and I held my lips tight together. He tried again, and I stiffened my body and held my lips even tighter. Truthfully, I did not know how to kiss, and I was not about to do parted lip kissing with him. He could not believe that at sixteen I didn't know how to kiss. He gave me a look of bewilderment and exited the door. I chuckled but had to admit he interested me. He visited a few more times, and for months we engaged in curious conversations on the phone, getting to know one another.

Meanwhile, I met Lil James, also from East Baltimore, who had a bronze hazelnut complexion and the facial features of a young James Brown with natural hair. Like Sylvester, he, too, was small-framed, short in stature, and a neat dresser. He was a smooth dancer but more so a talented singer who appeared destined for success in the entertainment world. Like James Brown, the "King of Soul," he was a dynamite showman. Additionally, he was blessed with a silver tongue and could talk as melodiously as he could sing. With perfection, he smooth-talked Minnie with schoolboy manners and expressive flattery every time he saw her. He could talk the fuzz off a peach and it was just peachy keen with her.

On the other hand, Minnie felt quite the opposite about Sylvester. He was polite but not overly friendly towards her. Based on what she knew of his reputation from her friends in Earnest Lyon Homes, he was considered to be a "bad news character." At 14 years old, he was a product of the streets: in fights or caught up in one hustle or another. He had twice been to Boys Village, a detention facility for juvenile males in Cheltenham, Maryland, but never shared with me the specific reason why. He only acknowledged being in the wrong place at the wrong time. Neither Minnie nor I believed that jive explanation.

For my own good, Minnie warned me not to "fool with that boy, Sylvester." Even my girlfriends preferred Lil James because of his characteristic likeability versus Sylvester's impulsive, controlling personality and quick temper.

My good friend and road buddy Rosetta (Boo) was adamant about me not seeing Sylvester. She told him face-to-face, "You are too domineering, and I know Beulah can do a lot better." He asked her jokingly what domineering meant, and she rolled her eyes and walked away.

Laura, my laid-back friend who very seldom disagreed with anything, in her slow drawl told me, "Beulah, I don't know about that Sylvester. I think he is too wild and crazy for a nice girl like you." I respected her opinion but, more importantly, she and I exchanged my once a week lunch money on Fridays for her bagged lunch of tuna fish salad sandwich, apple and cookies. Nobody seasoned, mixed, and stirred tuna fish like her mother, Miss Woodard. It was my weekly treat, and I was not sacrificing it or our friendship because of Laura's negative opinions concerning Sylvester. Leroy, my sixth-grade crush, also expressed disapproval of our relationship. He told Sylvester, "One day Beulah will become Mrs. Lewis, my wife, mark my words."

At the time, I was hanging out with William and Mack, who were both good-looking, and my special friend boys. I respected them both. William was brown-skinned and Mack deep dark. They both were tall with killer smiles like Sidney Poitier that brightened their personas to be even more handsome. Our friendship involved meeting up on the steps at my house, the corner of the Foster Grocery Bus, dances, and house parties. Although we talked about everything under the sun, when I mentioned Sylvester, William would only grunt, and Mack stayed silent. Grunts and silence spoke volumes.

I continued to see Sylvester because even with his outer toughness, I sensed his vulnerabilities. He shared with me that his "rock" of a mother, Miss Viola, had died suddenly after child birth of a hemorrhagic stroke when he was only 12. Her sudden passing away was just prior to the family relocating from Earnest Lyon Homes to a new home in East Baltimore. His aunt Octavia (Sis), Miss Viola's sister, and her husband, Josh, raised his infant brother, Reginald.

Sylvester's father, Mr. Levi, worked swing shifts at the Bethlehem Steel Corporation and partied with friends on weekends. He spent little time fathering Sylvester. Also, in the household were his older siblings: sisters Bertina and Erma; brother Bubbles; and grandmother Miss Clotel. Bubbles and Erma were self-motivated and focused on their academic achievements and ambitions. Being teenagers, they, too, had little time for Sylvester. Except for the love and support he received from Miss Clotel and his cousin Gwendolyn, fending for himself became the norm. Regrettably, he had not made the best decisions for himself and had to learn from the "school of hard knocks."

I knew Minnie, Boo, Laura, and Leroy were all looking out for me and meant well, but I did not share their point of view. Sylvester spoke in a natural loud bass voice, which was oftentimes mistaken to be argumentative, even in the calmest setting. Secondly, his animated expressions of finger pointing and hand movement while engaged in conversations with me and others were misconstrued by onlookers as domineering. Thirdly, I had a say in everything that happened between us, and, more often than not, our relationship centered on Sylvester going the extra mile to stay in my good graces, not me in his. Lastly, I believed that with my influence, I could get him to "change" and be more acceptable to Minnie and my friends. In other words, I thought him to be trainable. However, he was not about an exclusive relationship without "doing the do," and I felt totally the opposite. Several weeks passed with just telephone calls but no visits. I learned from my friend Josephine (Dean), who also lived on the Eastside, that he was preoccupied with pursuing other female interests: Sylvia and Reatha.

Mert put a bug in Sylvester's ear that Lil James and I were fast becoming a twosome, drawing circles, dancing at the "Y" on Friday nights and the Teen Center on Saturday nights. Sylvester unexpectedly dropped in at the "Y" to check out what the hype was regarding Lil James and me. While James and I were grinning and hand dancing, Sylvester came from out of nowhere, took my other hand, and did a couple steps/turns, winked, and walked away. It was an interesting night. As in several other instances, Lil James and his posse had to hightail it out of Turner Station as soon as the dance was over to avoid a beat down by the territorial fellows of Sollers Homes. Sylvester walked me home.

I continued for months seeing James and talking to Sylvester; however, achieving good grades in my eleventh-grade coursework was my number one priority. I found history with Mr. Howard Flournoy to be a delight. As with Mr. Woolfolk in tenth grade, he made boring past events jump off the history book pages with his profound but humorous sharing of the United States/world periods, people, and events. Mr. Flournoy was known for giving pop quizzes and tests without warning. After barely passing a few of them, I learned to review the subject matter nightly to be prepared for his "got you" surprises. My Uncle Coot had impressed upon me at the beginning of junior high school the importance of attaining good grades to open the door to future opportunities. I wanted more than anything to be accepted into the Marines with good standing so that I could achieve rank, benefits, and opportunities to travel the world.

The Sollers Point Junior-Senior Prom was held on Friday, May 1, 1959. Sylvester and I were becoming closer as boy and girlfriend, and we had great fun together. However, he was not interested in going to what he considered to be a "prim and proper lame dress-up dance," so Jimmy, my fun-loving buddy, took me. Jimmy and I had a sweaty dancing, gut laughing good time. Afterward, we continued partying into the wee hours of the morning at Flavia's parents', Mr. Biggie's and Miss Ruth's home. Their basement was a club room with a bar, booths, tables, and a dance floor. As far as I knew, it was the only house with a club room in Turner Station; it was swanky. Jimmy and I both were soaking wet after jitterbugging continuously into the wee hours of the morning. It was indeed "good morning" when he escorted me to my door, warmly hugged me, and pecked a kiss on my cheek. It was a night of fun I will never forget.

The following Friday, I was crowned "May Day Queen" as a result of receiving the majority vote of the junior class. I felt like

I was on cloud nine. As May Day celebrated the arrival of spring, I wore a pastel powder blue gown, carried a bouquet of mixed flowers, and was crowned with a jeweled costume tiara. It was a glorious sunny day of outdoor activities with the band playing, glee club singing, and dancers weaving in and out, wrapping colorful crepe paper around the May Pole. I intermingled with students throughout the campus. The entire student body was having a grand time, as were the faculty. It was a special day, and I felt so honored to be May Day Queen. I could not wait to write Momma and share it.

At the conclusion of the festivities, Sonny, my good buddy, congratulated me and innocently put his arm around my shoulder in a gesture of "so glad for you." As quick as lightning flashes, Miss Williams approached and sternly reprimanded us for improper conduct. She suspended both of us from school on the spot. Entertaining no "ifs or buts," she directed us to get off the school grounds immediately. I was shocked and embarrassed to the depth of my soul by the stares of disbelief from my fellow students. Adding insult to my hurt was having to walk the mile+ to Sollers Homes in my blue pastel gown in high heels with my tiara atop my head accompanied by Sonny, rightfully cussing all the way. We were in utter disbelief. Miss Williams was thought to favor students from the community of Sparrows Point and those in the academic curriculum, and we were neither. We chalked up this harsh treatment of us to our being from Sollers Homes. My expressed anger to Minnie landed on deaf ears. She regarded Miss Williams as a strict disciplinarian who sought the best from her students and did not challenge her.

Upon returning to school that Monday, Miss Williams further lowered our disheartened spirits with more insult by placing Sonny and me in detention for one hour after school for the entire week. I could not wrap my head around what I considered to be just plain meanness. During my five years at Sollers Point, unlike a few of her prima donnas whom she held in high esteem, as much as I desired to do so, I had never sneaked over to the Dog House, a popular carryout many students preferred over the cafeteria food. Even though the cheeseburger subs, hot dogs, and coconut custard pie were to die for, I at no time ventured beyond the school grounds or committed any infraction against school policy. Again, Minnie had no problem with what I considered Miss Williams' unfair disciplinary treatment of me.

Sylvester identified with my hurt and, in an attempt to make me feel better, took me on our first date to the movies that following Saturday. I took two transit busses, #10 and #13, and met him at his home in East Baltimore. From there, we walked about 13 city blocks to the Apollo Movie Theatre on Harford Road. For me, it was a long hike. Keeping up with Sylvester's fast, bouncy stride was like being in a relay race. However, I was happy to be clutching his arm, walking the streets, and seeing the sights of the city. People were friendly, and the houses were beautiful. I was awestruck by block after block of row houses with marbled white stoops and an array of sceneries painted on the window screens. By the time we arrived, I was winded and ready to slip my aching feet out of my shoes.

I do not remember the movie we saw, only that Sylvester put his arm around my shoulder as we ate popcorn and Good and Plenty candy and drank sodas. Sylvester later confided that it was his first date, too, and even though he had a pocket full of money, he had no clue how much I would eat; thus, he saved on bus fare. Other than him being frugal, there was no reason for us to walk back to his home, but we did. It was a sweet first date, ending with us riding the same two busses that I had traveled on earlier, hand in hand to Turner Station.

Our second date was a couple months later on a Friday night at the home of Sylvester's friend Joshua. It was a blue-light-in the-basement party with everybody jamming and sweating. All was well until Sylvester introduced me to Reatha, a recent ex-girlfriend. She expressed her dislike for me by rolling her eyes at both of us and walking away. Shortly thereafter, I was hand dancing with Mitchell, Sylvester's best friend, and Mitchell's brother, Billy, when I was kicked hard on my lower leg. Because of the overcrowded dance space on the floor and dark lighting, I first thought somebody was just dancing wildly. After two more such kicks during the next couple of records, I realized it was Reatha, intentionally kicking me.

Sylvester was nowhere to be found, and naïve church-going me was totally out of my "get along with everybody" Turner Station element. Thankfully, Beebe, who was well-respected in East Baltimore for being street savvy and able to hold her own in the midst of conflicting situations, had overheard Reatha saying, "I am going to kick her bony legs off her body before the night is over." Being that Beebe was a friend of Sylvester and my cousin Joan, she invited me to hang with her circle of friends for the rest of the party. Seeing that I was in the protection of Beebe, Reatha left me alone. I danced the night away kick free with not only Sylvester but also with Lil James and two of the most popular dancers in East Baltimore, Bay Boone and Lil Bill.

From time to time, talent shows were held at Sollers Point High in conjunction with special Friday night dances. Sylvester had told me that he would be performing that night with a band playing the guitar. I was hand dancing with Moses when I spotted Sylvester entering the auditorium. To my utter surprise, he had a conk hairstyle. I stopped dancing in the middle of the record to take a second and third look through the crowd. He had conked his hair with congolene, a hair straightener gel made from lye. His black hair was slicked back on his head with a big flat hussy curl in the center of his forehead. He was no Billy Eckstein. When I expressed my dislike for his new do, he shrugged it off with a wink and headed for the stage.

Once Sylvester was on stage playing the guitar with the band, he became the center of attraction, imitating the Chuck Berry duck walk. The crowd went wild with him plucking the strings of the guitar, stepping, shaking, and gyrating to the beat. I, too, was caught up with his performance and had to admit the conked hair added oomph to his act.

Over time, in spite of concerns from Minnie and close friends, a divine power within my being won out for Sylvester. It was like God had a plan of destiny for our lives. Likewise, Lil James was blessed with the absolute love of his life, Evelyn (Dee). A friendship between the four of us blossomed and became lasting.

In the summer of 1959, for the first time ever, I did not have a desire to go to Winston-Salem to stay with Momma. I wanted to spend my last summer with Sylvester and my friends before graduating and then joining the Marines, but Minnie insisted I go. Uncle Son visited for a week, and I returned to Winston-Salem with him by train. I was not a happy camper. Once there, selling snowballs and going to the park, movies, and church revivals were no longer exciting.

Momma being frugal, forbade me from calling Sylvester and most certainly refused his collect calls to me. About once a week, he called from home or his cousin Pi Jo's house for a few minutes to tell me that he missed me and what was going on with him. We often would be eavesdropped on or interrupted by folks sharing Momma's multiple telephone party line. An old busybody lady told Momma that she heard some boy saying he missed me and was waiting for the day I would return home. Momma was not surprised because she, too, snooped on our calls, and thought the relationship was becoming too serious for my 17 years. However, she knew there was nothing she could do about it.

To add some spice to my humdrum life, Momma allowed me to go see Jerry Butler (Iceman) and the Impressions with Miss Dora (choir member). It was my first show ever of that caliber: theatre, lights, entertainers in sharp suits, and a swooning crowd. All was well until Jerry sang "For Your Precious Love," which was Sylvester's and my love song. By the time Jerry Butler sang "And darling, they say that our love won't grow. But I just want to tell them they don't know. For as long as you're in love with me, our love will grow wider, deeper than any sea," I was crying tears like a waterfall running down my cheeks. Miss Dora was truly concerned by my uncontrollable display of emotion and told Momma to watch me because I definitely had the "hots" for some boy. I was some kind of missing Sylvester.

Once back home, all was well with Sylvester and me. The only drawback was that he was pressuring me to prove my love and commitment to him. I thought I loved him but was not ready to "do the do." One night in early winter, while walking home from Teen Center, he confessed his love for me. He later shared that seeing me in my "needing-a-cleaning, red, oversized coat with the seam loose under the right sleeve" pulled at his heartstrings. At that moment, he felt it was him and me against the world, and he cared for me more deeply than words could express. It was a lasting moment.

Unlike Minnie, her favorite uncle, David (Dave), Momma's baby brother, instantly liked Sylvester when they met. Uncle Dave supported our relationship and told us to make a house full of babies. He was a character. He visited us on Tompkins Court once a month on the weekend after receiving his check from the Veterans Administration. He had served in the United States Army as a Private First Class in World War II, driving a heavy-duty truck. Tours of duty took him to Normandy, France, and countries in Africa. His complexion was deep dark, he stood nearly six feet tall, and he weighed over two hundred pounds. He had a sizeable ugly scar on the back of his neck from being hit by shrapnel.

Uncle Dave was always neatly dressed in an expensive suit with a starched shirt, tie, Stetson hat, and Stacey Adams shoes; he looked like a preacher. He liked the fact that Sylvester mimicked him in his style of dress, from suits to shoes. The bus was his mode of transportation from West Baltimore to Turner Station. He generally kicked the door to alert us he was there because his hands were always full of grocery bags of food and several bottles of Wild Irish Rose Wine. Once settled in with a meal, quiet-mannered Uncle Dave would indulge in his wine. The more he drank, the more he reminisced and cried about two particular experiences on his tours of duty in France and Africa. One was about his relationship with a four-foot pygmy woman with whom he fell in love. The other was of him being awarded the Good Conduct and European-African-Middle Eastern Service Ribbon Medals.

Although married when he entered the service in 1943, Uncle Dave became romantically involved with a pygmy woman, and they became a couple accepted by others in the village. For the most part, they got along well. However, when she wanted no bother with him for whatever reason, she would climb a tree and stay up there for hours, ignoring his pleas for her to come down. The pain of having to leave her to return to the States left a lasting hurt in his soul. Uncle Dave would whisper "man talk" tidbits with Sylvester about the pygmy lady up the tree that would have him on the floor belly-roll laughing. The rest of us, including Minnie, were not privy to the nitty gritty of that particular story. Not once did I ever meet his wife, Magaline (Pauline, according to LuDella Currie, the Drake Historian), and I do not recall him ever mentioning her in his storytelling.

Porter loved Uncle Dave as we all did, but his repeated crying and drunken ramblings tried Porter's patience to where he either retreated to the bedroom or left the house. The more Uncle Dave drank, the more he talked, cried, and passed out one-dollar bills to us kids. We too would belly-roll laugh when he showed us how the pygmies danced, spreading his big feet apart, slow stepping, bouncing, clapping his hands, and popping his fingers, all the while singing in an unknown language. Once Sylvester went home, Jackie, Bay Bay, Cedric, Carole, and I were his captive audience. He was relentless, following us into our bedroom and talking and crying until we fell asleep. I knew he loved us, but sometimes he got on my last nerve with his nonstop talking and crying. When sober he was totally the opposite; quiet and reserved, a treasure of a gentleman. After several occasions of Sylvester being amused by Uncle Dave's wine drinking, storytelling, and crying, Sylvester affectionately began referring to him as "Cry Baby Uncle Dave" and that nickname became our little secret.

In the twelfth grade, I persevered studiously and continued with my God-given social ease of dealing with students, teachers, Mr. Fletcher, Miss Williams, and other staff. I was voted Miss Sollers Point 1959-1960 by the school body much to the dissatisfaction of Miss Williams. She ruled the election void and called for a second election without the seventh and eighth graders (a first). She believed I had an unfair advantage because those particular junior high classes were heavily concentrated with students from

Sollers Homes. Regrettably, even though I made Minnie aware of what I perceived to be yet again unfair treatment of me by Miss Williams, my "strong take no stuff" mother did not confront her on my behalf. She simply believed if it were to be, I would win without the votes of the lower grade schoolmates.

The second election festivities in the school auditorium were full of apprehension among students as to what the outcome would be. Would I win or would I lose? The boys who performed on the corners on summer nights under the light poles sang the latest hits with lyrics substituted to showcase a particular contestant prior to our short speeches and the voting. Foball's group rearranged "Get A Job" lyrics by the Silhouettes to "Vote for Beulah" to introduce me. Their harmonizing and dance moves to the beat of "Yip yip yip yip yip yip yip yip, Sha na na na, sha na na na na, Vote for Beulah, Sha na na na, sha na na na na" had the entire auditorium of students on their feet. Prior to the crowning, we five candidates were lined up at the entrance of the stage, and I was on the end. As Mr. Lawrence Custis, vocational shop teacher, approached the podium with the results to announce the winner, he whispered in my ear, "You still got it hands down." He had not been pleased with the decision to redo the vote and had voiced his opinion of unfairness to Miss Williams' deaf ears.

With much fanfare, Mr. Custis declared Beulah Mae Newton Miss Sollers Point of 1959-1960, with John D. Powell as my escort, and the celebration began with "Shout" by the Isley Brothers. I was on the floor circled by most of the student body "getting down" when Mr. Fletcher and Miss Williams approached. As they stood among the students, she pointed to me and sarcastically said "and that's Miss Sollers Point." In response to her sarcasm, I gyrated to the floor, rocking it in the low crouch position on the refrain "You know you make me wanna (Shout-woo) hey-yeah, (Shout-woo) yeah-yeah-yeah, (Shout-woo) all-right, (Shout-woo) all-right, (Shout-woo) come on now!" Mr. Fletcher and Miss Williams walked away in a huff, and I felt redeemed.

My most important responsibility as Miss Sollers Point was to represent Sollers at Morgan State College's Homecoming that October along with the other local high school queens. To ensure that I would be dressed appropriately, Miss Williams requested that I bring my complete outfit in for her approval (probably another first). I was not pleased in being asked to do so and took her request as a personal affront.

I called Momma to tell her of my being chosen to represent my school at Morgan State. She was so happy and proud. She wired by Western Union more than enough money to buy the perfect ensemble. So much in fact that Minnie and I bypassed her frequently shopped, reasonably priced Epstein's and Goldberg's department stores in East Baltimore and continued on the transit bus to downtown Howard Street, the hub of the more expensive stores. We bought a stylish blue plaid suit, hat, gloves, and shoes from the intermediate priced but fashionable Brager-Gutman's. Miss Williams readily gave her approval of my outfit and the pretty beige coat that I borrowed from my cousin Maxine. I represented Sollers in an impressive fashion much to Miss Williams' delight.

As I continued in my twelfth-grade classes, sewing in home economics with Miss Johnson became even more satisfying than in her previous classes. I made a wool top and skirt ensemble and coordinated it with a lace scarf, gloves, and hat. I wore my outfit to St. Matthew, and nobody believed it was my own creation. Under the teaching of Miss Johnson, I learned the economic value of being able to make or alter my own clothes and the importance of them being well-fitted. Likewise, my first-time homemade rolls were delicious. Without permission from Miss Young, the culinary teacher, I took two rolls home for Minnie to taste. Her approval was important to me because she was the best in baking light, buttery, melt-in-your-mouth rolls. Our Sunday dinners always included hot rolls, greens, potato salad, my fried chicken, and Jackie's three-layer chocolate or vanilla cake.

Drivers Education with Mr. Robert Patterson was an unforgettable experience. I did well with classroom safe driving instruction and thought driving would be a piece of cake. I was so wrong! Actually, driving a car and interacting with other drivers along Erdman Avenue in East Baltimore, our main practice route, was a far cry from book learning. After maneuvering one near miss here or there, I got the hang of it and really appreciated Mr. Patterson for his patience and nerves of steel. It was a challenge, but I passed the class.

To my surprise, I loved English/literature with Miss Williams. She was an exceptional teacher. Through her keen ability to give life to the historical backdrops and characters being studied, I was able to connect to the readings and be in the moment. Particularly interesting was the series on William Shakespeare. I often quoted "To be, or not to be" from *Hamlet* and *Romeo and Juliet's*, "O' Romeo, Romeo, wherefore art thou Romeo?" Elizabeth Barrett Browning's poem, "How Do I Love Thee?," was my absolute favorite because it touched my heart. I committed it to memory and quoted it to Sylvester so frequently that he could recite it back to me. We both appreciated its meaning of intense love.

My frequent literary interactions with Miss Williams allowed her to view me in a more positive light. She appeared to soften her preconceived labeling of my being from Sollers Homes. Our respect and appreciation for one another improved over the course of the year, and I did extremely well in her class.

Pumpkin Seeds of Thanks

During my senior year, I served on the student council and literature committee of the yearbook staff. I was also assistant secretary for the senior class, president of 12B C classes, and a member of the dance group.

Unfortunately, I was one of the few students who failed to pay class dues timely. The monies were for my personalized yearbook, class ring, cap, and gown. The week of the due date, Miss Williams asked me on Monday, on Tuesday, on Wednesday, and on Thursday for the money. She told me that I would not be allowed to attend commencement or receive my diploma unless I paid by the next day, Friday. In all my negative dealings with her, for the first time, I understood her standpoint and held no hard feelings toward her. I blamed Porter.

As I dressed for school that Friday morning, I was full of dread knowing I still had not received the money from Momma. I had called her earlier in the week when it became apparent that Porter would not be able to pay it. However, my precious supportive Momma, whom I needed more than ever, was not physically well enough to transact the money transfer at the Western Union office, and nobody was available to do so for her. I was in wait. At no less than four blocks from the school, I made a decision to hook school for the first time in my life. I could not endure the embarrassment of having to face Miss Williams without my class dues for the fifth day.

The family of my close friends Annie and Edna had moved from Sollers Homes to West Baltimore. Without calling, I rode two transit busses to their house, hoping that Annie, who had recently dropped out of school because she was expecting a baby that September, would be home. Lucky for me, Annie was there; her siblings were in school. Miss Sherrod was out of state visiting family. Annie and I talked and giggled the day away with plates of greasy salted french fries floating in ketchup and drank a pitcher of cherry Kool-Aid. All my troubles were forgotten. We had a ball. Without a doubt, if Miss Sherrod had been home, she would have called Minnie and sent me packing. However, with Annie and Edna being teenagers like me, they welcomed my visit as a girlfriend get-together. I spent the night with them without ever letting anybody know of my whereabouts, not even Sylvester.

Upon learning I had not shown up for school, Porter and Minnie were franticly worried. Minnie knew I was upset about not being able to pay my class dues but did not believe it was to the extent that I would deliberately hook school. Once she made contact with Sylvester, expecting me to be with him, and learned he had not heard from me that entire day, emotions of dread overtook her. She broke down crying and called the police. I was missing without a trace.

In the interim, Sylvester searched the bush areas all around Sollers Homes, hoping not to find me. The degree of anxiety I was causing everybody never once dawned on me. I was so caught up in my own pity party. I returned home late on Saturday evening to the relief and welcoming arms of Minnie and Porter, who forgave my unauthorized stay with the Sherrods. Western Union had delivered. Monday could not come fast enough!

Commencement was on Sunday, June 12, 1960, Minnie's 37th birthday; she was six months with child. As the class marched proudly into the auditorium on "War March of the Priests from Athalia" by Felix Mendelssohn, I glimpsed Porter and Minnie in the audience and became emotional and teary. A flood of mixed feelings engulfed the depth of my soul as sentimental memories danced through my mind. I was a couple of hours away from never walking those polished halls again; seeing my close friends, associates, and caring teachers; being chastised by Miss Williams;

singing our alma mater "Sollers Point, Oh! Sollers Point"; and not socializing or dancing after school to Ransom's jukebox.

Miss Williams assisted in the awarding of diplomas by calling the roster of names. I still hear her distinctively stretching every syllable of Beulah Mae Newton. I literally hated my first and middle names. At the conclusion of the ceremony, I, with my head held high, recessed to the "Choral Procession" by Richard Kountz. It was heart-rending. My Sollers Point foundational experience was complete.

Hugs, kisses, well wishes, and farewells were followed by the after-party at the home of Reginald's (Reggie's) aunt in West Baltimore on a small street off of Edmondson Avenue and Poplar Grove. Reggie drove us in his creme-colored 1957 Plymouth Fury with his girlfriend, Margie, upfront. Betty, Mamie, Jimmy J, Sylvester, and I sat in the back with two of us girls sitting on the guys' laps like glued puzzles.

The entire block of Reggie's Aunt's welcoming neighbors was amused as we excited graduates stiffly rolled out of the car looking like actors in a slapstick comedy. As the party ended around midnight, we dared not go home because we would break the traditional graduation all-nighter rite of passage. We happily drove around until the break of day, reminiscing about fun times, mimicking the teachers, and recalling the unpleasant encounters with Mr. Fletcher and Miss Williams. One classmate (not a passenger in our car), who shall remain nameless, did not return home for a week.

Thus, my Sollers Point Junior-Senior High School experience was complete. Many of my academic friends, including Flavia, were accepted to attend college at Bennett, Coppin, Lincoln, Maryland State (Eastern Shore) or Morgan State. Others who had taken the commercial curriculum were bound for Cortez Peters, the first Colored professional, clerical, and business school. With jobs being plentiful at Bethlehem Steel, General Motors, Western Electric, Westinghouse, and the government, many students obtained local employment or joined the armed services; such was not the case for me. To my dismay, I did not walk across the stage alone. My dreams of becoming a Marine and fulfilling the Criterion Yearbook's class prophecy of becoming a Major General would never materialize. Deep down inside of me, I anxiously embraced a life-changing secret, a lack of innocence, and a sense of unknowns for what the future held. A new, unplanned life was dawning. What a time, what a time!

"Pumpkin Seeds of Thanks" to God for His covering through the heartbreak of losing my precious Uncle Coot; for the extraordinary blessing of my beloved Momma, Porter, Minnie, and siblings; for allowing me to survive the hard knocks of being a low self-esteemed teenager and disappointments in adolescence; for finding true love with Sylvester; for matchless good times with family and friends; for my six years of educational achievement at Sollers Point Junior High School; for instilling in me the will to persevere in spite of being a stutterer; and for the caring faculty and staff who laid the groundwork for my determination to be fruitful in the not-so-inviting real world called life.

Hallelujah to God for all of my *"Pumpkin Seeds of Thanks!"*

Miss Sollers Point

Rocking Through Challenges

Beulah Newton
Miss Sollers Point High

The Miss Sollers Point Contest is an event that the entire school awaits each year. As a result of this occurrence, a senior is chosen Miss Sollers Point. This young lady represents the school at the annual Morgan State College Homecoming Game.

This year, 1960, Miss Sollers Point High is Beulah Newton. Beulah represented the school very well, leaving her new acquaintances made at Morgan with a very favorable impression of her, and hence of Sollers Point High School. Escorting Miss Newton is a fellow classmate, John Powell.

First Cabaret

Night Out